ACT® 5-Hour Quick Prep

**by Lisa Zimmer Hatch, MA,
and Scott A. Hatch, JD**

for
dummies®
A Wiley Brand

ACT® 5-Hour Quick Prep For Dummies®

Published by: **John Wiley & Sons, Inc.,** 111 River Street, Hoboken, NJ 07030-5774, www.wiley.com

Copyright © 2024 by John Wiley & Sons, Inc., Hoboken, New Jersey

Published simultaneously in Canada

For general information on our other products and services, please contact our Customer Care Department within the U.S. at 877-762-2974, outside the U.S. at 317-572-3993, or fax 317-572-4002. For technical support, please visit https://hub.wiley.com/community/support/dummies.

Wiley publishes in a variety of print and electronic formats and by print-on-demand. Some material included with standard print versions of this book may not be included in e-books or in print-on-demand. If this book refers to media such as a CD or DVD that is not included in the version you purchased, you may download this material at http://booksupport.wiley.com. For more information about Wiley products, visit www.wiley.com.

Library of Congress Control Number: 2023947198

ISBN 978-1-394-23163-8 (pbk); ISBN 978-1-394-23165-2 (ebk); ISBN 978-1-394-23164-5 (ebk)

SKY10063508_122923

Table of Contents

Start Here

Welcome to *ACT 5-Hour Quick Prep For Dummies*. The goal of this book is to show you exactly how to survive the ridiculous situation called the ACT. No one wants to deal with a standardized test for too terribly long. This book has one goal: to help you prepare for the ACT as quickly and painlessly as possible.

About This Book

You likely can't escape the ACT. Many colleges require you to take this entrance exam before they'll even look at your application. Virtually every college accepts scores from either the ACT or the SAT. (Wiley just so happens to publish *SAT 5-Hour Quick Prep For Dummies* as well, should you choose to take that exam.)

In *ACT 5-Hour Quick Prep For Dummies*, you find five study blocks that add up to five hours. Depending on how much you know about each subject and how fast a test-taker you are, each block might take a little more or a little less time than promised, but the time promise does give you a good idea of how much time to set aside for each study block so you pace yourself and show up for the ACT as sharp as a no. 2 pencil.

Some study blocks are short and others are long, depending on what you're trying to accomplish. Here's a rundown of what you'll find in each block and about how much time it takes to complete:

» **Block 1 (20 minutes):** Find out what you need to know about registering for the ACT, exam rules and tips, the topics covered, and ACT scoring.

» **Block 2 (1 hour, 15 minutes):** Discover the question types you find on each test and content-specific knowledge you'll need to know.

» **Block 3 (45 minutes):** Take closer look at the question types you find on each test and review detailed explanations of the answers.

» **Block 4 (2 hours, 30 minutes):** This block contains an abbreviated practice test. By taking this practice test, you'll understand how to pace yourself, what content you need to review, and so on before you take the real ACT.

» **Block 5 (10 minutes):** The shortest block in the book offers quick tips to review the night before you take the ACT.

Foolish Assumptions

We're betting you picked up this book because you have to take the ACT. (Isn't it good to know at the outset that your authors have a remarkable grasp of the obvious?) And because we weren't born yesterday, we figure that

» You're taking the ACT in anticipation of applying to college. How exciting for you!

>> Getting the best ACT score you can is important to you and you care enough to sacrifice some of your free time to achieve that goal. Good for you!

>> You're busy and you don't want us to waste your time with a bunch of stuff that isn't on the ACT. For instance, we don't share vocabulary flashcards with you in this book because you don't need to memorize word meanings to ace the ACT.

>> You've spent some years engaged in a secondary school curriculum and you've written an essay or two. Therefore, we don't bore you too much with elementary stuff but do cover the basic math and grammar concepts that you may have forgotten.

Icons Used in This Book

Some information in this book is really, really important. We flag it by using an icon. Here's a list of the icons we use and details about what they mean:

Follow the arrow to score a bull's-eye by using the tips we highlight with this icon.

Burn this stuff into your brain or carve it into your heart; it's the really important material. If you skip or ignore the Remember icons, you won't get your money's worth out of this book.

Pay heed to this advice and avoid the potential pitfall.

Where to Go from Here

We suggest two ways to use this book:

>> **Fine-tune your skills.** Maybe you're already a math whiz and you just need help with the English grammar. Go right to the English review in Block 2.

>> **Start from scratch.** Grab a sack of food and some sharpened pencils, lock yourself in your room, and go through this book word for word. It's not as bad as it seems, and starting from scratch is the preferred method. Many students make what we call the "mediocre mistake": They're good at one section, mediocre at a second, and dismal at another. They spend all their time in their worst section and barely look at the sections that they're mediocre or good in. Big mistake! A couple of points that you gain in your mediocre section are just as valuable as — and a heck of a lot easier to get than — the same number of points you gain in your weakest section. Humor us and read the book from cover to cover. You'll pick up some great material.

Whichever way you progress through the blocks, absolutely take the practice test in Block 4. To use the practice test, we suggest two tried-and-true methods:

>> **Diagnostic:** Take the practice exam first to see how you score. Then devour the subject reviews and advice we provide in Blocks 2 and 3.

>> **Pure practice:** Devour the reviews and advice first and use the full-length exam to practice and reinforce what you've learned in the rest of the book.

Block 1
ACT Overview in 20 Minutes

I n a nutshell, the ACT is designed to test what you learned in high school (or secondary school if you're outside the United States) and how well you can apply critical thinking and analysis skills to what you read — or numerical problems in the case of the math test. Your score on the ACT helps admissions folks at colleges and universities understand how well prepared you are for college-level work.

Of course, it's more than a little weird to judge everything you learned over about four years into about four hours. But that's the task before you, and you give yourself an advantage if you have some idea of what to expect on the ACT.

In this block, you get the facts about signing up for the test, including how to request accommodations if you're eligible. You find out what to bring, what rules you have to follow during the exam, and some basics about the ACT format. You also find pointers about understanding your score and what to do if you didn't score as well as you'd hoped.

Registering for the ACT

If your school has a day when all students take the ACT, the school probably takes care of your registration for you.

However, if you want or need to take the SAT on your own, you need to know when you want to take the test and plan far in advance if you need to request accommodations for a learning disability, English learner accommodations, or a fee waiver. You must have certain details and documentation ready when you register, so read on to find out how to make all this paperwork go smoothly.

Choosing when to take the test

Currently, the ACT is offered at testing sites nationwide and internationally on weekends every February, April, June, July, September, October, and December. Additionally, some school districts offer the ACT during the school day in March, April, October, and November, depending on the high school. If you live in a district that offers one of these schoolday tests, your test date is set for you, but all other options allow for a little freedom of choice.

The best time to take the ACT is not a one-size-fits-all consideration. You may want to wait to take the test until you feel most prepared, but you also need to give yourself plenty of time to retake the test before you apply to college. Most colleges don't require you to send the scores from every time you take the ACT, so you don't necessarily have to be completely prepared before you take your first official test. Also, many colleges allow you to superscore your ACT scores, which means they'll consider only your highest English, math, reading, and science scores from all the times you take the ACT. In fact, the ACT even creates a superscore score report if you take the test more than once. Therefore, there's not a major downside to taking the test sooner rather than later.

Generally, if you've taken algebra II and trigonometry during your sophomore year, we suggest that you consider taking your first ACT test in the first semester of your junior year in either September, October, or December. (If you're taking algebra II and trig during your junior year, you may want to wait until February or April of your junior year to take the first test.) The beauty of testing in the fall of your junior year is that you can devote the summer before to extensive ACT study.

TIP

A perk of taking the December test is that it offers Test Information Release (TIR), which means you can pay extra to get a copy of your test questions and a report of the ones you answered correctly and incorrectly. This valuable information can come in handy when preparing for subsequent tests. This service is also available for the April and June exams.

If you take the test in the fall, you have plenty of options to retake the ACT in the spring and summer to achieve your top score. You can even get some extra summer study time in during the summer before your senior year and take the September ACT. Your scores from this test should be available in plenty of time before the earliest application deadlines in October and November. If you postpone taking your first ACT until April or June of your junior year, you may not have enough retakes to optimize your score.

Table 1-1 summarizes these scenarios to help you choose when to take the ACT.

TABLE 1-1   When to Take the ACT

If You Take Algebra II and Trig at This Time	Then Take Your First ACT at This Time	Pros	Cons
Sophomore year	Fall of junior year	Time to study over the summer and more time to improve your score	None
Junior year	Spring of junior year	Better prepared for the math test	Less time overall to improve your overall score

Deciding whether to take the writing test

The ACT provides an optional Writing Test in addition to the other four multiple-choice sections. Its importance in the college application process is dwindling, and most colleges don't require or even recommend it. If you need to write the essay to enhance your application, make sure you present your best effort, as explained in Block 2.

Asking for accommodations or English learner supports

Not everyone takes the ACT under the same conditions. You may have a special circumstance that can allow you to change the date of the ACT or the way you take your exam. Here are a few of the special circumstances that may affect how you take the ACT:

>> **Learning disabilities:** If you have a diagnosed learning disability (LD), you may be able to get special accommodations, such as more time to take the test. However, you must specifically request such accommodations way in advance. Prepare your requests for fall tests by the prior June and for spring tests by the prior September. Please note that in order to be eligible for special testing on the ACT, your LD must have been diagnosed by a professional, and you should have a current individualized education plan at school that includes extended test time. Talk to your counselor for more information. Note that you can only request special accommodations in conjunction with a test registration.

>> **Physical disabilities:** If you have a physical disability, you may be able to take a test in a special format — in Braille, large print, or on audio. Go to the official ACT website (www.act.org) for complete information about special testing.

>> **Religious obligations:** If your religion prohibits you from taking a test on a Saturday, you may test on an alternate date. The ACT registration website specifies dates and locations in each state.

>> **Military duty:** If you're an active military person, you don't complete the normal ACT registration form. Instead, ask your Educational Services Officer about testing through DANTES (Defense Activity for Nontraditional Educational Support).

>> **English language learner:** In the United States, if you aren't proficient in English, the ACT enables you to apply for English learner supports. Because these supports expire yearly, you have to apply for the accommodation each year you take the ACT. English language learners must submit documentation of their status, such as WIDA or TOEFL scores or an official accommodations plan. If your request for English language learner supports is approved, you may be eligible for extended time, a word-to-word dictionary, directions in your native language, or small group testing. The ACT registration website explains how to apply for these accommodations and provides more details.

Requesting a fee waiver

In the United States, Puerto Rico, and U.S. territories, you can request a fee waiver. The fee waiver means you don't have the pay to take the ACT, which currently costs about $60 to $85, depending on whether you take the optional writing test. Your school counselor can help you understand whether you're eligible or you can read the information at www.act.org. If you qualify, you can take the ACT up to four times for free and receive free learning resources. You'll receive a fee waiver code that you enter when you sign up for the test.

Signing up for your test

To register for the ACT, you need about 30 minutes and the following items:

» A computer with Internet access

» Credit card or other payment

» High school course information

» Headshot photo

REMEMBER

If you need accommodations, English learner supports, or a fee waiver, read those earlier sections before you register so you get the resources you're entitled to.

When you're ready, go to www.act.org. Choose Start Your Journey Here ⇨ Take the SAT as shown in Figure 1-1. You need to create an account or sign in and then follow the prompts online to register.

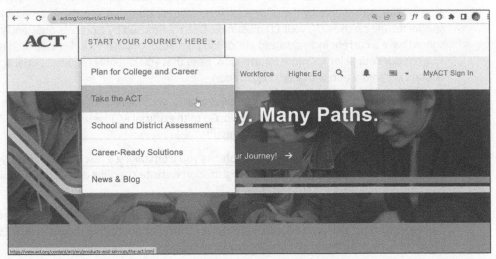

FIGURE 1-1: Signing up for the ACT online.

Identifying What to Bring to the Test

If you can't borrow the brain of that whiz kid in your calculus class for the day, you're stuck using your own. To compensate, be sure that you have the following with you before you leave for the ACT test center:

» **Admission ticket:** You receive your ticket immediately after you register online. Be sure to print it out so you have it for test day.

» **Pencils:** If you take the ACT in the United States, the ACT is a paper test. Take a bunch of sharpened No. 2 pencils with you. You may also want to take good erasers (nothing personal — everyone makes mistakes). Mechanical pencils aren't allowed.

» **Map or directions:** Go to the test center a few days before the actual exam to scope out your driving route and parking area. Often, the ACT is given at high schools or colleges that have parking lots far, far away from the test rooms. Drive to the location a few days in advance, park your car, and see just how long it takes you to get to the room. You don't need the stress of having to run to the test room at the last minute on test day.

>> **Clothing:** Schools that host the ACT often turn off the heat for the weekend (the ACT is usually offered on a Saturday), and the test room can be freezing cold. Alternately, in the summer, schools turn off the air conditioning, making the room boiling hot. Dress in layers and be prepared for anything.

>> **Photo ID:** Showing the birthmark your boyfriend or girlfriend thinks is so cute isn't going to cut it with the test proctor. You need to upload a photo when you register for the test and bring a photo ID (student ID, driver's license, passport, military ID, FBI Most Wanted mug shot, whatever) to the exam. If you don't have a photo ID, you can bring a letter of identification. The form is available on the official ACT website (act.org).

>> **Eyeglasses:** Students taking the ACT frequently forget their reading glasses at home and then squint for the four long hours of the test. The ACT is enough of a headache on its own; you don't need eyestrain, as well. If you wear contacts, be sure to bring cleaning/wetting solution in case you have to take the lenses out and reinsert them during the break. (Hey, all those tears can really mess up your lenses!)

>> **Snack:** True, you get only one 10-minute break between the Math and Reading Tests, but that's enough time to gobble down something to jump-start your brain. We often suggest taking an energy bar or some peanuts, something with protein and carbohydrates. Scarfing down a candy bar is actually counterproductive; your sugar levels rise only momentarily and then drop down below where they were before you had your chocolate fix.

>> **Watch:** Keeping track of time on your own timepiece is more efficient than wasting precious seconds seeking out the clock on the testing site wall. Place your watch on the desk where you can refer to it easily throughout the exam. Digital watches or smartwatches may not be allowed. Stick with ones that have faces and hands. Your watch can't make any sounds either. If the proctor hears so much as a beep from your watch, she will not-so-politely request that you leave the building and cancel your test.

>> **Calculator:** The ACT gurus allow you to use a calculator only on the Mathematics Test. Although the ACT information bulletin has an entire quarter page detailing which calculators you can and cannot use, generally, you can use any calculator (yes, even a graphing calculator) as long as it doesn't make a noise or have a computer algebra system. Make sure the one you bring has at least a square root function and, ideally, basic trigonometry functions. You may not use a laptop computer (don't laugh; you'd be surprised by how many students want to bring one to the test!).

Knowing What to Expect During the Test

Have you ever been so excited about something only to watch all those expectations melt into a big puddle of disappointment? This is how our friend's daughter felt when her significant other broke up with her right before prom. (But she ended up having a great time after all!) Expectations are often a great setup for disappointment, but when you're taking the ACT, having some expectations is helpful. You'll know what you're getting yourself into.

This section helps you understand the exam room rules; the order, topics, and time for each test; and what the ACT thinks you should know to be prepared for college.

Exam room rules

The ACT is pretty strict about what is and isn't allowed in the exam room. Do not, we repeat *do not*, take any of the following items with you to the ACT test room:

» **Cellphones and other electronic devices:** Leave your cellphone in the car. You aren't allowed to bring it into the test room. One student we know was dismissed from the test because he accidentally left his cellphone in his pocket, and it rang during the exam. The same goes for other electronics, such as iPads, PC tablets, or anything else that can access the Internet or make a sound.

» **Books and notes:** Take it from us: Last-minute studying doesn't do much good. So leave all your books at home; you aren't allowed to take them into the test room with you. (Just be sure to fill your parents in on this rule. We once had a student whose mother drove all the way to the test center with her daughter's ACT prep book, thinking the girl needed it for the test. The mom actually pulled the girl out of the test to give her the book, resulting in the girl's nearly being disqualified from the test.)

» **Scratch paper:** You may not bring your own scratch paper to the paper-based test, and you don't receive any scratch paper during the exam. Fortunately, the exam booklet has plenty of blank space on which you can do your calculations.

When you're done with one test, know that you're done. You can't go back to a previous section and finish work there or change some of your answers. If you try to do so, the proctor will catch you and you'll be in a world of hurt.

One last rule that you should already know: Cheating on the ACT is a loser's game — it's just plain stupid. Apart from the legal, moral, and ethical questions, you can't predict what types of grammatical mistakes will show up in the questions; what are you going to do, copy a textbook on the palm of your hand? All the math formulas that you need can't fit onto the bottom of your shoe.

The order, topics, and time for each section

The ACT is actually four tests in one — or five in one if you take the optional writing test. The test for each subject follows the same order, and you can expect to see a certain number of questions, certain topics, and have a certain amount of time for each test. Table 1-2 gives you the bird's-eye view of what to expect in each section of the ACT.

TABLE 1-2   ACT Breakdown by Section

Test	Number of Questions	What They're About	Time Allotted
English	75	Most are about English usage and mechanics. About 15% ask you to identify and eliminate redundant language. About 25% ask about writing skills like organization, style, and strategy	45 minutes
Mathematics	60	About one-third of the questions are arithmetic, one-third are algebra, and one-third are geometry.	60 minutes

Test	Number of Questions	What They're About	Time Allotted
Reading	40	You will read 4 passages, which include 1 passage and 10 questions for each of the following topics: literary narrative social studies humanities natural sciences	35 minutes
Science	40	You will read 6 passages and answer 6-7 questions per passage. 2-3 passages about data representation 2-3 passages about research summaries 1 passage about conflicting viewpoints	35 minutes
Writing (optional)	1	Your ability to state, analyze, and evaluate the perspectives given as well as your own, using relevant supporting details. Throughout your essay, you should organize your ideas, maintain focus, and communicate your ideas clearly.	40 minutes

If you add up the numbers, you find that you have 216 multiple-choice questions to answer in 215 minutes; 215 minutes is 3 hours and 35 minutes, or just over 3.5 hours. You get one 10-minute break between the second and third tests (the Mathematics and Reading Tests). You may also encounter an extra 20-minute section after the Science Test that the ACT will use to determine the difficulty of questions for later exams. If you choose not to take the optional Writing Test, you get to walk out right after that. If you include the time in the classroom spent giving out the tests, explaining the directions, checking IDs, answering the Interest Inventory questions, and so on, your whole morning is shot. You may as well figure on giving up 4 to 4.5 hours for this test.

What the ACT expects you to know

The ACT tests the following subjects:

>> **English:** The ACT expects you to know the fundamentals of grammar, usage, punctuation, diction, and rhetorical skills. For example, you must understand sentence construction — what makes a run-on and what makes a fragment. You need to know how to distinguish between commonly confused words, like *affect* and *effect* or *principal* and *principle*. You must be able to use the proper forms of words, distinguishing between an adjective and an adverb, and you must know the difference between a comma and a semicolon. Block 2 addresses the English portion of the test.

>> **Mathematics:** The ACT requires basic skills in arithmetic, geometry, and algebra. If you've had two semesters of algebra, two semesters of geometry, and a general math background, you have the math you need to answer about 90 percent of the questions. The ACT also tests algebra II and trigonometry. Oh, and you don't have to know calculus. The ACT has no calculus questions. Happy day! Refer to Block 2 for more.

>> **Reading:** The ACT expects you to be able to read a passage in a relatively short amount of time and answer questions based on it. Although you probably don't have time to significantly improve your reading skills before you take the ACT, you can still improve your ACT Reading score. Block 2 shows you a few tricks you can use to improve your speed and tells you how to recognize and avoid traps built into the questions.

THE COMPUTER-BASED ACT

If you take the ACT in a country other than the United States, your exam is offered on computer rather than on paper. This computerized option has been available for several years and may become more common at testing sites in the United States.

The question types, numbers of questions, and scores are the same whether you take the paper or computer-based version of the ACT; the only difference is in the method of delivery. The computer-based ACT, or CBT, provides handy tools that allow you to approach it in much the same way you would for the paper test:

- **Highlighter and line reader:** Use these tools to focus on important data and sentences.
- **Answer eliminator and masker:** Use these tools to help you mark out wrong answers.
- **Magnifier:** This tool allows you to read the fine print for charts and graphs in the science questions.

You also have a timer to keep track of your time and the ability to move between questions and mark them for later review.

The ACT had plans to expand the digital version of the ACT and make it more widely available throughout the United States, but those plans have been delayed indefinitely.

>> **Science:** You don't have to have much specific science background to ace the Science Test. The passages may test chemistry, biology, botany, physics, or any other science, but you don't have to have had those courses. The test gives you all the information you need to answer most of the science questions in the passages, diagrams, charts, and tables. Head to Block 2 for more about the Science Test.

>> **Writing (optional):** The ACT folks added this optional section to test your writing ability. Don't worry! You've been writing for years, and the ACT people know that you can't possibly write a perfect essay in a measly 40 minutes. They're not focusing on perfection; instead, they're looking at your thesis, organization, and ability to support your thoughts. The ACT doesn't require you to write the essay, and few colleges require or even recommend the essay. The essay portion of the ACT may be eliminated from the test entirely in future administrations. Block 2 gives you the lowdown on the Writing portion of the ACT.

Identifying Strategies for Test-Taking Success

On the wall of our office, we have a padded cushion that's imprinted with the words, "BANG HEAD HERE!" We've found that most of our students use it either to reduce stress or express their exasperation over careless mistakes. To avoid becoming a head-banger, read the material in this section about how to relax and avoid common mistakes.

Managing your time

Every section on the ACT begins with directions and a line that tells you exactly how many questions are in the section and, therefore, how many minutes you have per question. The ACT is no big mystery. You can waste a lot of time and drive yourself crazy if you keep flipping pages and counting up how many more questions you have to do. You can do what you can do; that's all. Looking ahead and panicking are counterproductive and waste time.

The ACT contains a few incredibly hard questions. Forget about 'em. Almost no one gets them right, anyway. Every year, a ridiculously small number of students receive a score of 36, and if you get into the 30s, you're in a superelite club of only a few percent of the thousands and thousands of students who take the ACT annually. Just accept the fact that you either won't get to or can't answer a few of the hard questions and learn to live with your imperfection. If you do go quickly enough to get to the hard questions, don't waste too much time on them. See if you can use common sense to eliminate any answers. Then mark your best guess from the remaining choices.

REMEMBER

Every question counts the same in a section, whether that question is a simple $1 + 1 = 2$ or some deadly word problem that may as well be written in Lithuanian.

Keeping track of your answers

Suppose that you decide to postpone doing Question 11, hoping that inspiration will strike later. But now you accidentally put the answer to Question 12 in the blank for Question 11 . . . and mess up all the numbers from that point on. After you answer Question 40, you suddenly realize that you just filled in Bubble Number 39 and have one bubble left — *aaargh!*

TIP

To avoid having to re-answer all the questions, thank your lucky stars that you bought this book and took the following advice: When you choose an answer, *circle that answer in your test booklet first* and *then* fill in the answer on the answer grid. Doing so takes you a mere nanosecond and helps you not only in this panic situation but also as you go back and double-check your work. If you have a good eraser with you (and you should), the wrong answers on the answer grid should take only a few seconds to erase.

Coping with stress and anxiety

Most people are tense before a test and often feel butterflies dancing in their stomachs. The key is to use relaxation techniques that keep your mind on your test and not on your tummy. To avoid becoming paralyzed by a frustrating question during the test, we suggest that you develop and practice a relaxation plan (perhaps one that includes the techniques we describe in the following sections). At the first sign of panic, take a quick timeout. You'll either calm down enough to handle the question, or you'll get enough perspective to realize that it's just one little test question and not worth your anguish. Mark your best guess and move on. If you have time, you can revisit the question later.

TIP

Practice a quick relaxation routine in the days before you take the exam so that you know just what to do when you feel panicky on test day. Here are some suggestions:

>> **Inhale deeply.** Restore the steady flow of oxygen to your brain by inhaling deeply. Feel the air go all the way down to your toes. Hold it and then let it all out slowly. Repeat this process again several times.

>> **Stretch a little.** Scan your body for muscle tension and stretch these areas to get the blood flowing. You can shrug your shoulders toward your ears, roll your head slowly in a circle, stretch your arms over your head.

>> **Think positive thoughts.** Any time you notice yourself thinking negative thoughts, make a conscious effort to change the script. For example, "I got most of this math right; no sense worrying now. Overall, I think I'm doing great!"

Eliminating answers

Facing a set of four answer choices in the hope that the correct one will reveal itself can be daunting. Instead of searching for the one correct answer in the bunch, focus on wrong answers. You'll usually have an easier time finding something wrong with an answer. The key is to reject choices based on careful analysis rather than a gut feeling.

Usually, two of the four (or for math questions, three of the five) answer choices will be relatively easy to identify as wrong. They will obviously be off topic or contain specific information that the passages or questions don't address. When you're deliberating between the two remaining options, look for problems with one of the answers. Sometimes just one word will make the answer incorrect. The correct answer is the one left standing after you've found problems with the others.

Reading actively to stay focused

When you're in the middle of an excruciatingly boring reading passage, the worst thing you can do is let your mind drift off to a more pleasant time. Even if you have to pinch yourself to keep from falling asleep or flaking out, stay focused. A less painful option is writing a keyword next to each paragraph in the passage so you're reading actively. For example, if a paragraph is about lab test results, you might write keyword or phrase that reflects the findings.

Reviewing your responses

Mark in your test booklet questions you're unsure about as you work through a section. If you finish a test early, go back and double-check the *easy* and *medium* marked questions. Don't spend more time trying to do the hard questions. If a question was too time-consuming for you five minutes ago, it's probably still not worth your time. If you made a totally careless or dumb mistake on an easy question, however, reviewing the problem gives you a chance to catch and correct your error. You're more likely to gain points by double-checking easy questions than by staring open-mouthed at the hard ones.

REMEMBER

Every question counts the same. A point you save by catching a careless mistake is just as valuable as a point you earn, grunting and sweating, by solving a mondo-hard problem.

Understanding Your Score

As a future ACT test-taker and current reader of this book, we're guessing you care very much about your score. This section explains how individual questions are scored, your ACT score report, and what you need to know about repeating the test to improve your score.

Guessing for points to maximize your score

Scoring on the ACT is very straightforward:

>> You get one point for every answer you get right.

>> You get zero points for every answer you omit.

>> You get zero points for every answer you get wrong.

REMEMBER

The ACT doesn't penalize you for wrong answers. Therefore, guessing on the ACT obviously works to your advantage. Never leave any question blank. We suggest that you save a couple of seconds at the end of each section just to go through the test and make sure that you've filled in an answer for every single question.

Interpreting your overall score

We once had a frustrated student tell us that the scores on the ACT looked a lot like measurements to him: 34, 29, 36. However, the ACT has four scores, which makes for a very strange set of measurements! The ACT scores are nothing like high school scores based on percentages. They're not even like the familiar SAT scores that range from 200 to 800. Instead, they range from 1 to 36. You can see an example score report in Figure 1-2.

Average of Math, Science, English, and Reading scores

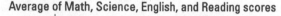

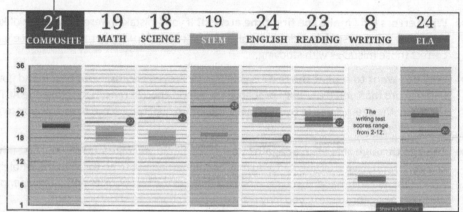

FIGURE 1-2:
An example
ACT score
report.

Scoring on the ACT works like this:

>> Each required test (English, Mathematics, Reading, and Science) receives a *scaled score* between 1 (low) and 36 (high).

>> The *composite score* is the average of the four required test-scaled scores.

>> If you take the ACT Plus Writing (which is the official title for the ACT with the optional Writing Test), you receive a Writing score that ranges from 2 (low) to 12 (high). The score is the sum of the average of each of the four subscores you receive from each of the two people who grade your essay. The Writing Test score is completely separate from your composite ACT score.

>> You may see additional readiness indicators that colleges will see but that aren't combined in any way with your ACT composite. Here's a quick look at what they mean:

• A STEM Score represents overall performance on the math and science sections.

• An English Language Arts Score combines your performance on the English, Reading, and Writing Tests.

• The Progress Toward Career Readiness Indicator measures your progress toward career readiness for a variety of careers.

• The Understanding Complex Tests indicator tells you whether you're sufficiently understanding text material for college and career level reading.

>> A *percentile score* tells you where you rank in your state and nationwide.

Look at the percentiles. Just knowing that you got a 26 doesn't tell you much. You need to know whether a 26 is in the 50th percentile, the 75th percentile, or the 99th percentile. If you get a 36, you have documented lifetime bragging rights because that's a perfect score!

To see a complete sample score report, visit the ACT website (www.act.org). The sample shows you what all these scores look like when you and your colleges of choice receive them.

Repeating the test to improve your score

Are you allowed to repeat the ACT? Yes. Should you repeat the ACT? Probably. Other than the additional cost (both financial and emotional) required to test again, there is no real downside to retesting. Decide whether you want to repeat the ACT based on your answers to the following questions:

>> **What errors did I make the first time around?** If your mistakes were from a lack of knowledge, that is, you just plain didn't know a grammar rule or a math formula, you can easily correct those mistakes with studying.

>> **Why do I want to repeat the test?** Is your ego destroyed because your best friend got a better score than you did? That's probably not a good enough reason to retake the ACT. Do retake the exam if you're trying to get a minimum qualifying score to enable you to get into a college or earn a scholarship.

>> **Can I go through this all over again?** How seriously did you take studying the first time around? If you gave it all you had, you may be too burned out to go through the whole process again. On the other hand, if you just zoomed through the test booklet and didn't spend much time preparing for the test, you may want a second chance to show your stuff.

>> **Were my mistakes caused by factors that were not my fault?** Maybe you were in a fender-bender on your way to the exam, or perhaps you stayed up late the night before in an argument with your parents or your best friend. If you just weren't up to par when you took the exam, definitely take it again, and this time be sure to get a good night's sleep the night before.

If you take the ACT in a national administration in April, June, or December, you can pay to see a digital copy of your full ACT test and the questions you missed. This handy resource gives you valuable information to study for a future test. The cost for this Test Information Release (TIR) is $30 when you register for the test, and access to the test questions is available as soon as you receive your scores for that ACT test date. You can order TIR after you receive your scores, but it'll cost you $40. This service is only available for April, June, or December test dates in the United States. This feature isn't offered for international administrations of the test.

The ACT doesn't automatically send colleges the scores for every time you take the test. It gives you the option of deciding which set of scores you want colleges to see. If you don't want to report the results of all your tests, keep these issues in mind:

>> **The ACT automatically sends scores to the colleges you list on your test registration form.** If you want to wait until after you see your report to decide whether certain colleges can see your scores for a particular test administration, don't list those colleges with your ACT registration.

>> **Many colleges figure your ACT composite score by averaging the highest scores you get in each section across all administrations of the test.** They refer to this practice as *superscoring* the ACT. If you get a 24 in English, a 21 in Math, a 23 in Reading, and a 25 in Science the first time you take the ACT and a 25, 20, 24, and 24, respectively, the second time, these colleges will figure your composite score by averaging your higher 25 English score, 21 Math score, 24 Reading score, and 25 Science score. Your composite score for each administration would be 23, but the composite score the colleges calculate would be 24. Therefore, you may want the colleges to get reports from all the times you take the ACT so that they can superscore your highest section scores. When the ACT institutes section retesting and the superscore report, your highest section scores will appear on one report, and (if colleges allow), you'll only have to send (and pay for) one report.

>> **A handful of colleges require you to report your scores from every test date.** Check with the admissions committee at the colleges to which you're applying to make sure they allow you to withhold score reports from particular test dates.

REMEMBER

A growing number of colleges allow you to self-report your ACT scores. Those colleges consider the ACT scores you list on your college applications or report within the college's online portal, depending on the policies of the individual school, to make admissions decisions. You only send an official score report after you've been admitted to and have decided to attend that particular college. Self-reporting allows you to save the money you'd have spent to send official score reports to every college on your application list. If you're able to take advantage of the self-reporting option, be sure to follow the college's procedures exactly and report your scores accurately. A discrepancy between the scores you report on your application and the scores that appear on your official report could be grounds for rescinding your college acceptance.

Block 2
Preparing for the Test!

To be ready for the ACT, you need to know what's on the test and get some tips for responding for the seemingly endless questions you must answer in a short amount of time. In other words, this block helps you put on your game face before you walk into the exam room. You'll know what you need to know, or if you're not sure of the answers, you'll have some strategies for getting through it.

Punctuating the English Test

When you open your ACT booklet, the first thing you see is the English Test. Your still half asleep brain and bleary eyes encounter 5 passages and 75 questions. Somehow, you're to read all the passages and answer all the questions within 45 minutes. That may seem like a lot of questions in a little bit of time, but the English questions really aren't super time-consuming.

The questions on the English Test fall into the following three categories:

>> **Conventions of Standard English (CSE):** A little more than half of the questions cover English usage and mechanics. These questions include sentence structure, grammar and usage, and punctuation. See "Reviewing grammar and usage" later in this block for more details.

>> **Knowledge of Language (KLA):** The questions that ask you to eliminate unnecessary or redundant expressions comprise about 15 percent of the English Test. By practicing with the example questions in Block 3 and the practice test in Block 4, you'll learn to spot repetitive language almost instinctively.

>> **Power of Writing (POW):** About a quarter of the questions test writing skills, such as organization and relevance (reordering the sentences or adding sentences to the passage), style (which expression, slang or formal, is appropriate within the passage or which transition properly joins two thoughts), and strategy ("Which answer most specifically conveys what Grandpa likes to eat for supper?").

The ACT English Test passages look like standard reading-comprehension passages — but these passages have many underlined portions. An underlined portion can be an entire sentence, a phrase, or even just one word. The five passages cover a variety of topics, and one type of passage is not necessarily more difficult than another. Although the English test passages aren't reading-comprehension passages per se, you do need to pay at least a little attention to content instead of just focusing on the underlined portions because a few questions ask you about the purpose of the passage or what a possible conclusion might be.

Understanding the question types

Most of the test is about analyzing answer choices and then choosing which answer fits best in the place occupied by underlined words in a sentence. Your job is to determine what type of error the question tests and which of the choices provides the correct expression.

Approach these types of questions methodically:

1. **Look at the answer choice options listed in the right column for clues to the type of error the question tests.**

Errors to look for include pronoun or punctuation problems, word choice issues, redundancy, and subject/verb agreement mistakes.

2. **Eliminate answer choices that contain errors.**

3. **Reread the sentence with the answer you've chosen inserted.**

Don't skip this step. You may overlook a problem with your answer until you see how it works in the complete sentence.

A few of the questions in the English Test ask you to strategize about content, style, and organization. These questions usually come right out and ask you a question about the passage. The best way to approach these questions is by eliminating answer choices that can't be right.

Sometimes the answer to a question is a simple yes or no. So first, you decide whether the answer to the question is yes or no. Then you choose the answer that provides the best reason for the yes or no answer. See Block 3 for an example.

Reviewing grammar and usage

Because more than half of the ACT English test is questions about conventions of standard English, you'll benefit from brushing up on English grammar and usage.

Parts of speech

Most of the English Test questions ask you to evaluate sentences. Every word in a sentence has a purpose, known as its *part of speech.* The parts of speech you should know for the ACT are verbs, nouns, pronouns, adjectives, adverbs, conjunctions, and prepositions. If you need more information to understand any of the material covered here, check out Grammar Girl's resources about the parts of speech at www.quickanddirtytips.com/articles/parts-of-speech.

VERBS

A sentence must have a *verb* to be complete. For the ACT, make sure you know these concepts about verbs:

> >> **The difference between an action verb and a linking verb:** *Action verbs* state what's going on in a sentence. *Linking verbs,* such as the verb *to be,* link one part of the sentence to the other, sort of like the equals sign in an equation.

>> **The distinction between a verb's different forms:** The infinite form is *to* + the verb (*to run* or *to be*). The conjugated form changes depending on the subject (*I run, he runs*). The participle form helps other verbs as part of a verb phrase (*He is running, they have run*).

>> **The types of verb tenses:** The most important verb tenses to know for the test are present, past, future, present perfect, and past perfect tenses.

NOUNS

You've undoubtedly heard *nouns* defined as persons, places, things, or ideas. In a sentence, nouns can have different roles, such as subject, direct objects, indirect objects, objects of prepositions, and predicate nouns. In this sentence, for each italicized noun, see if you can identify its type:

> The social studies *teacher* gave the *students* five *pages* of *homework* regarding *countries* in *Europe* and asked them to write an *essay* on the political *consequences* of *joining* the *European Union*.

The subject is *Teacher*. Direct objects are *pages*, *essay*, and *European Union*. An indirect object is *students*. Objects of prepositions are *homework, countries, Europe, consequences,* and *joining*. The sentence doesn't have any predicate nouns.

PRONOUNS

Pronouns rename nouns and provide a way to avoid too much repetition of nouns in a sentence or paragraph. To answer English Test questions on the ACT, get familiar with these types of pronouns:

>> **Personal pronouns rename specific nouns.** They take several forms: subjective (*I, she*), objective (*me, her*), possessive (*my, her*), and reflexive (*myself, herself*).

>> **Demonstrative pronouns point to nouns.** Words like *some, many, both, that, this, those,* and *these* when they're not paired with a noun can also serve as pronouns. (*That* is my favorite book.)

>> **Relative pronouns connect descriptions to nouns.** Relative pronouns include *that, which,* and *who* (the subjective form), *whom* (the objective form), and *whose* (the possessive form). These pronouns are the subjects of descriptive clauses; *who* is the subject of clauses that describe persons, and *which* and *that* refer to entities that aren't people. Clauses that start with *which* are always nonessential (and therefore are set off with commas), and clauses that start with *that* are essential.

ADJECTIVES

Adjectives describe and clarify nouns. In the sentence "The putrid odor in the lab resulted in a bunch of sick students," *putrid* defines the kind of odor and *sick* describes the condition of the students. Without the adjectives, the sentence takes on a different and ridiculous meaning: The odor in the lab resulted in a bunch of students.

TIP

When you check a sentence on the exam for errors, make sure the adjectives are in the correct places so that each adjective describes the word it's supposed to.

ADVERBS

Adverbs give extra information about action verbs, adjectives, and other adverbs. They include all words and groups of words (called *adverb phrases*) that answer the questions where, when, how, how much, and why. In the sentence "The chemistry students gradually recovered from smelling the very putrid odor," *gradually* explains how the students recovered.

REMEMBER

You may see a question that asks for the best placement of an adverb. The most logical position for an adverb in the sentence is cozied up to the action verb it describes.

CONJUNCTIONS AND PREPOSITIONS

Conjunctions and *prepositions* link the main elements of a sentence. These often seemingly inconsequential words can play a major role in English Test questions. Here is what you need to remember:

» **Conjunctions join words, phrases, and clauses.** Coordinating conjunctions include *and, but, for,* and *so.* Correlative conjunctions always appear in pairs, like *neither/nor.* Subordinating conjunctions introduce dependent clauses and include *although, because, before, if, unless, when,* and *while.* Don't worry about memorizing these terms; just know that they exist.

» **Prepositions join nouns to the rest of the sentence.** We'd need several pages to list all the prepositions, but common examples are *about, above, by, for, over,* and *with.* Prepositions always appear in prepositional phrases, which also include a noun. Prepositional phrases usually describe a noun (the students *in the band*) or a verb (the football player ran *down the field*).

Parts of a sentence

The parts of speech we describe in the preceding section work together to form sentences. Every sentence and clause has two parts: the subject and the predicate.

» The subject is the main actor in the sentence; it's the noun that's doing the action in the sentence or whose condition the sentence describes.

» The predicate is the verb and pretty much everything else in the main idea of the sentence that isn't part of the subject. The part of the predicate that isn't the verb is called the *complement.* The complement can be an adjective, predicate noun, direct object, or indirect object.

A sentence also usually contains single words, phrases, or clauses that convey more information about the sentence's main message. *Phrases* and *clauses* are groups of words that work together to form a single part of speech, like an adverb or adjective. The difference between phrases and clauses is that clauses contain their own subjects and verbs; phrases don't.

The two types of clauses are independent and dependent:

» **Independent clauses express complete thoughts and can stand as sentences by themselves.** The sentence "Jeff opened the door, and the cat slipped out" contains two independent clauses.

» **Dependent clauses express incomplete thoughts and are, therefore, sentence fragments if left by themselves.** "Although the cat slipped out" is an example of a dependent clause. To convert any dependent clause into a complete sentence, you must add an independent clause, as in "Although the cat slipped out, Jeff caught it before it could run away."

REMEMBER

Understanding the difference between independent and dependent clauses helps you recognize errors, such as sentence fragments, reference issues, and punctuation problems.

Punctuation rules

You use periods, commas, semicolons, and other forms of punctuation all the time when you write. But are you using them correctly? The ACT English Test gives you questions to make sure you know how. Punctuation rules are pretty straightforward. After you have them down, you can be sure you're practicing proper punctuation.

TIP

The following sections briefly explain what you need to know for the ACT. If you need to review any of these rules more in-depth and test your knowledge with a practice quiz, go to Khan Academy (http://www.khanacademy.org) and search for lessons on punctuation and the specific mark. For example, type **punctuation semicolon** in the search box.

PERIODS AND QUESTION MARKS

The ACT rarely tests marks that end the sentence, but just in case, here's what you need to know about periods and question marks. Periods end sentences that aren't questions (like this one). Question marks end direct questions, like "When will dinner be ready?" However, you never put a question mark at the end of indirect questions, such as "Pam asked me when dinner would be ready."

SEMICOLONS

The semicolon links two independent clauses in one sentence. Using semicolons is appropriate in the following instances:

» **To join two independent yet closely related clauses without a conjunction:** For example, the sentence "It's almost the weekend; I can finally relax."

» **To begin a second clause with a conjunctive adverb:** Clauses that begin with conjunctive adverbs (such as *accordingly, also, besides, consequently, furthermore, however, so*) use a semicolon to separate them from another clause. For example: "I should relax this weekend; otherwise, I'll be tired all week."

» **To provide clarity in complex sentences:** Semicolons appear in sentences that have a numbered series or when using commas would be confusing. The ACT rarely tests this use for semicolons.

COLONS

Colons have several functions. You can use them in place of periods to separate two independent clauses (although semicolons usually fill this role). You can also use them to relate the introductory clause in a sentence to a relevant list of specifics, a long appositive or explanation, or a quotation. Here's an example: "Megan will be finished with her homework when she completes these three tasks: a rough outline for an essay, a worksheet of math problems, and the final draft of her chemistry report." For the ACT, the only rule you need to consider when evaluating colons is that they must be preceded by a complete independent clause.

COMMAS

The comma is perhaps the most misused punctuation mark in the English language. Whenever you see an underlined comma in the English Test, evaluate its purpose. Here are a couple of important general rules to keep in mind when you encounter commas on the ACT:

» **Don't put a comma in a sentence just because you think it needs a pause.** Pausing is subjective; comma rules for the ACT aren't. You may pause between *cow* and *on* in this sentence to emphasize just how whacky the image is: *I saw a cow, on a bike!* But the ACT wouldn't agree with you. That comma is wrong. Use the rules that follow in this section (not your ears) to justify whether a comma is placed properly.

» **Remember that a single comma *never* separates a subject from its verb or a verb from the rest of the predicate.** A comma never comes between a prepositional phrase and the noun it describes. You may see *a pair* of commas between the subject and verb, but not a lone comma without a comma buddy.

Remember these comma uses to take the guesswork out of placing commas:

» **Series:** In a series of three or more expressions joined by one conjunction, put a comma after each expression except the last one, as in the sentence "Rachel, Bryan, and Tyler bought sandwiches, fruit, and doughnuts for the picnic." Notice that no comma comes after *Tyler* and no comma comes before *doughnuts*.

The ACT won't test whether you put a comma before the *and* in a series because there isn't a firm rule about that.

» **Omitted *and*:** Use a comma to replace an omitted *and* from a sentence in certain circumstances. For example, "I studied with Jerry yesterday, with Pam today."

» **Separation of clauses:** Use commas to join together clauses in these situations:

- Put a comma before a coordinating conjunction that joins two independent clauses. Here's an example: The polka-dot suit was Sammie's favorite, but she didn't wear it when she was feeling shy.

  A run-on sentence happens when a sentence with two or more independent clauses has improper punctuation. Here's an example: "I had a college interview yesterday morning and I'm pretty sure I knocked the interviewer's socks off." If you're confused about the error here, review run-ons on Khan Academy.

- Use a comma to set apart a beginning dependent clause from the rest of a sentence, as in "When Sammie feels shy, she doesn't wear her polka-dot suit."

» **Nonessentials:** When a sentence includes information that's important but not crucial to the meaning of the sentence, you set off that information with commas on both sides (unless the nonessential info begins or ends a sentence — then you just use one comma). Sometimes determining whether an expression is essential is difficult. If you don't know the rules for commas and the following situations, review that information online: asides, appositives, titles and distinctions, Latin abbreviations, dates and place names, nonrestrictive clauses and restrictive clauses. For example, the following sentence follows several of these rules:

"In my opinion, Georgia White, RN, the first speaker for today, should give her presentation in the Grand Ballroom, which has the red double doors, and share her speech on Friday, June 26, in Boulder, Colorado, to open the other major nursing conference."

To quickly review some comma rules, see Grammar Girl's comma chart at www.quickand dirtytips.com/articles/how-to-use-commas-a-summary.

DASHES

Dashes work like colons to introduce long appositives or like commas to designate nonessential information. They can separate a beginning series from the rest of a sentence and signal abrupt breaks in the continuity of a sentence. Here's an example: A state championship, a college scholarship, and a Super Bowl ring — such were the dreams of the high school quarterback.

APOSTROPHES

Apostrophes have two purposes — creating contractions and forming possessives. The apostrophe takes the place of the missing letter or letters in a contraction. Think *they're* (they are), *can't* (cannot), *here's* (here is), and so on.

To show ownership of one noun by another, use an apostrophe. For example, a dog owned by a girl is "the girl's dog" and an opinion of a judge is "a judge's opinion."

REMEMBER

None of the possessive pronouns contains an apostrophe. (*It's* is a contraction of *it is*, not the possessive form of *it*.) But indefinite pronouns do contain apostrophes, as in the sentence "Somebody's dog chewed my carpet."

Sizing Up the Math Test

Okay, you math whiz, here's a question for you. Quick, without your calculator, answer this question: How many seconds are there in a year? Answer: Exactly 12: January 2nd, February 2nd, March 2nd . . .

You can't escape the one-hour ACT Mathematics Test, no matter how hard you try. It's one of the four tests of the ACT. Although the math questions aren't as much fun as the ones we ask here, don't worry. This section tells you what you need to know to ace the test.

Because we've promised to help you prepare for this test in about five hours, this section focuses on the most common math questions and the details that you may have forgotten if you haven't used them recently. In practice, this means you won't find details about basics (like how to add and subtract or what parallel lines are) or infrequently asked topics (like advanced trig or matrices). But what if your math knowledge is not-so-common? If a topic isn't covered in depth but could appear on the test, we do identify what to look up in order to make this Quick Prep approach work for your specific needs.

Understanding the test format

The Mathematics Test is a 60-minute test and features 60 questions (which makes figuring out your average time per problem convenient, no?). The questions fall into pretty standard categories.

REMEMBER

The following is the short 'n' sweet version of the kinds of math questions you encounter in the dark alleyways of the ACT:

>> **Pre-algebra:** (Normal people refer to this as *arithmetic*.) Quite a few questions cover basic arithmetic, including such concepts as fractions, decimals, and subtracting negative numbers.

>> **Elementary algebra:** You learn this type of material in your first semester or two of algebra. These questions test your ability to work with variables, set up algebraic formulas, solve linear equations, and do the occasional FOIL problem.

>> **Intermediate algebra/coordinate geometry:** Fewer than half of the questions cover more difficult quadratic problems, as well as inequalities, bases, exponents, radicals, basic graphing (finding points on an *x, y*–coordinate graph), and functions.

>> **Probability and statistics:** A few of the questions expect you to know how to solve problems involving average/mean, median, combinations, permutations, and probability.

>> **Plane geometry and trigonometry:** Many questions cover plane figures (what you think of as "just plain figures," like triangles, circles, quadrilaterals, and so on), and trigonometry. The trig questions make up no more than 10 percent of the test, so if you haven't had trig yet, don't despair. At least half of the trig questions are very basic, covering trig ratios and basic trigonometric identities.

Recognizing number basics

The questions on the ACT that ask about the basic math topics we cover in this section tend to be the easiest, so they offer you the best chance for getting correct answers. Brush up on your elementary and middle school math, and you're sure to improve your score on the ACT Math Test. This section doesn't cover elementary math (like how to do addition, subtraction, multiplication, and division), but it does cover basic concepts and terms that are valuable to know on the ACT but easily forgotten.

Numbers fall under a hierarchy of classifications and are defined as such. Familiarize yourself with these terms so they don't trip you up on the test:

>> **Complex:** All numbers you can think of.

>> **Imaginary:** Represented by the variable i, the value of the square root of a negative number. Every once in a while, the ACT spits out a question that deals with an imaginary number. Just keep in mind that $i^2 = -1$ and $i = \sqrt{-1}$.

>> **Real:** All complex numbers that aren't imaginary. So when a question tells you to "express your answer in real numbers," don't sweat it. That's almost no constraint at all, because nearly every number you know is a real number.

>> **Irrational:** Numbers that can't be written as fractions, such as π and $\sqrt{2}$.

>> **Rational:** All real numbers that aren't irrational and therefore include fractions and decimal numbers that either end or repeat. For example, the fraction $\frac{1}{6}$ is a rational number. It can also be expressed as $0.1\overline{6}$.

>> **Integers:** All the positive and negative whole numbers, plus zero. Integers aren't fractions or decimals or portions of a number, so they include –5, –4, –3, –2, –1, 0, 1, 2, 3, 4, 5, and continue infinitely on either side of zero. Integers greater than zero are called *natural numbers* or *positive integers;* integers less than zero are called *negative integers.*

REMEMBER

Tread carefully when working with zero. It's neither positive nor negative.

>> **Whole:** All the positive integers and zero.

>> **Natural:** All the positive integers, excluding zero.

Absolute value

The concept of absolute value crops up quite a bit on the ACT. The *absolute value* of any real number is that same number without a negative sign. For example, the absolute value of 1 is written mathematically as $|1|$. Because 1 sits one space from zero on the number line, $|1| = 1$. But because –1 also sits one space away from zero on the number line, $|-1| = 1$.

REMEMBER

Absolute value relates only to the value that's inside those absolute value bars. If you see a negative sign outside the bars, the value of the result is negative. For example, $-|-1| = -1$.

Equations with a variable inside absolute value signs usually have two solutions: the one when the value within the signs is positive and the one when the value is negative.

$$|-3+x|=12$$
$$-3+x=12$$
$$x=15$$
$$|-3+x|=12$$
$$-(-3+x)=12$$
$$3-x=12$$
$$x=-9$$

Prime numbers and factorization

The ACT expects you to know about *prime numbers*, which are all the positive integers that can be divided only by themselves and 1. A number that can be divided by more numbers than 1 and itself is called a *composite number*. Here are some other facts you should know about prime numbers:

>> 1 is neither prime nor composite.

>> 2 is the smallest prime number and the only number that's both even and prime.

>> 0 can never be a prime number because you can divide zero by every number in existence, but it's not considered to be a composite number either.

TIP

You don't need to memorize all the prime numbers before you take the ACT (yikes!), but do keep in mind that the lowest prime numbers are 2, 3, 5, 7, 11, 13, 17, 19, 23, and 29.

When you know how to recognize prime numbers, you can engage in *prime factorization*, which is just a fancy way of saying that you can break down a number into all the prime numbers (or *factors*) that go into it (refer to Figure 2-1). For instance, 50 factors into 2 and 25, which factors into 5 and 5, giving you 2, 5, and 5 for the prime factors of 50:

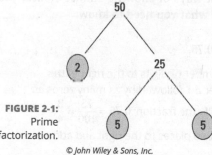

FIGURE 2-1:
Prime
factorization.

© John Wiley & Sons, Inc.

Distributive property of multiplication

For the ACT, you need to know is the *distributive property* of multiplication. You can multiply a number by a set of added or subtracted values by distributing that number through the values in the set values, like so:

$$2(3+4)=$$
$$(2\times3)+(2\times4)=$$
$$6+8=14$$

Of course, you can solve this problem by adding the numbers in parentheses $(3+4=7)$ and multiplying the sum by 2 $(7 \times 2 = 14)$. But when you start to add variables to the mix, you'll be glad you know about distribution.

Odds/evens and positives/negatives

The ACT may ask questions that require you to know what happens when you perform operations with odd and even numbers, as well as positives and negatives. *Even numbers* are numbers that are divisible by 2 (2, 4, 6, 8, 10, and so on), and *odd numbers* are numbers that are not divisible by 2 (1, 3, 5, 7, 9, 11, and so on). The easiest way to figure out operations with odds and evens is to try them with sample odd and even values.

To perform basic math operations with positive and negative numbers, remember these rules:

>> When you multiply or divide two positive numbers, the answer is positive.

>> When you multiply or divide two negative numbers, the answer is also positive.

>> When you multiply or divide a negative number by a positive number, you get a negative answer.

You also have to know a thing or two (or three, actually) about adding and subtracting positive and negative numbers:

>> When you add two positive numbers, your answer is positive: $3 + 5 = 8$.

>> When you add two negative numbers, your answer is negative: $-3 + -5 = -8$.

>> When you add a negative number to a positive number, your answer can be positive or negative: $-3 + 5 = 2$ and $3 + (-5) = -2$.

Converting fractions, decimals, and percentages

Because fractions, decimals, and percentages are different ways of showing similar values, you can change pretty easily from one form to another. Here's what you need to know:

>> To convert a fraction to a decimal, just divide: $\frac{3}{4} = 3 \div 4 = 0.75$.

>> To convert a decimal back to a fraction, first count the number of digits to the right of the decimal point. Then divide the number in the decimal over a 1 followed by as many zeros as there were digits to the right of the decimal. Finally, simplify the fraction: $0.75 = \frac{75}{100} = \frac{3}{4}$.

>> To change a decimal to a percent, just move the decimal two places to the right and add a percent sign: $0.75 = 75\%$.

>> To turn a percent into a decimal, move the decimal point two places to the left and get rid of the percent sign: $75\% = 0.75$.

Basic operations with fractions

Fractions tell you what part a piece is of a whole. The *numerator* is the top number in the fraction, and it represents the piece. The *denominator* is the bottom number of the fraction, and it indicates the value of the whole. If you cut a whole apple pie into 10 pieces and eat 5 slices, you can show the amount of pie you eat as a fraction, like so: $\frac{5}{10}$.

The ACT expects all fraction answers to be in their simplest forms. To simplify a fraction, first find the largest number you can think of that goes into both the numerator and denominator (called the *greatest common factor*). Then just divide the numerator and denominator by that number. For example, simplify $\frac{5}{10}$ by dividing the numerator and denominator by 5: $\frac{5}{10} = \frac{1}{2}$.

Multiplying fractions is easy. Just multiply the numerators by each other and then do the same with the denominators. Then simplify if you have to. For example,

$$\frac{3}{4} \times \frac{2}{5} = \frac{3 \times 2}{4 \times 5} = \frac{6}{20} = \frac{3}{10}$$

Before you multiply fractions, check whether you can cancel out any numbers to avoid simplifying at the end. In the preceding example, you can reduce the 4 and cancel the 2, leaving you with

$$\frac{3}{{}_{2}\cancel{4}} \times \frac{\cancel{2}^{1}}{5} = \frac{3 \times 1}{2 \times 5} = \frac{3}{10}$$

To divide fractions, find the *reciprocal* of the second fraction in the equation (that is, turn the second fraction upside down). Then multiply (yes, you have to multiply when dividing fractions) the numerators and denominators of the resulting fractions. For example,

$$\frac{1}{3} \div \frac{2}{5} = \frac{1}{3} \times \frac{5}{2} = \frac{5}{6}$$

Adding and subtracting fractions can be a little tricky, but you'll be fine if you follow these guidelines:

>> **You can add or subtract fractions only if they have the same denominator.** Add or subtract just the numerators, like so:

$$\frac{1}{3} + \frac{4}{3} = \frac{5}{3}$$

$$\frac{3}{8} - \frac{2}{8} = \frac{1}{8}$$

>> **When fractions don't have the same denominator, you have to find a common denominator.** To find a common denominator, you can multiply all the denominators, but you end up with some humongous numbers. Instead, find the lowest common denominator.

To find the lowest (or least) common denominator, think of multiples of the highest denominator until you find the one that all denominators go into evenly. For instance, to solve $\frac{4}{15} + \frac{1}{6}$, you have to find the lowest common denominator of 15 and 6. If you count by 15 ($15 \times 1 = 30$, $15 \times 2 = 30$), you might quickly realize both 15 and 6 go into 30, so 30 is the lowest common denominator.

You can use your graphing calculator to find the lowest common denominator (also known as the least common multiple, or LCM) for two or more numbers. Apply the *lcm* function, enter the set of numbers, and press Enter.

Here's a trick for working with fractions with variables. Multiply the denominators to find the lowest common denominator. Then cross-multiply to find the numerators.

Say you're asked to solve this problem:

$$\frac{a}{b} - \frac{c}{d} = ?$$

Find the common denominator by multiplying the two denominators: $b \times d = bd$. Then cross-multiply:

$$a \times d = ad$$
$$c \times b = cb$$

Put the difference of the results over the common denominator:

$$\frac{ad - cb}{bd}$$

A *mixed number* is a whole number with a fraction tagging along behind it, such as $2\frac{1}{3}$. To add, subtract, multiply, or divide with mixed numbers, you first have to convert them into *improper fractions* (fractions in which the numerator is larger than the denominator). To do so, multiply the whole number by the denominator and add that to the numerator. Put the sum over the denominator. For example,

$$2\frac{1}{3} = \frac{(2 \times 3) + 1}{3} = \frac{7}{3}$$

Percentages

REMEMBER

The ACT usually asks you to find a percentage of another number. When you get a question like "What is 30% of 60?" evaluate the language like so:

>> *What* means *?* or *x* (the unknown) or what you're trying to find out.

>> *Is* means = (equals).

>> *Of* means × (multiply).

Your job is to convert the words into math, like so: $? = 30\% \times 60$.

To solve this problem, convert 30% to a decimal (0.30) and multiply by 60. Tada! The answer is 18.

Sometimes a problem asks you to figure out what percent one number is of another. For example, the number 20 is what percent of 80? To solve this type of problem, use the preceding translation guide to get a math equation you can work with: 20 equals *x* times 80, or 20 = 80*x*. To solve for *x*, divide both sides by 80, and you get $\frac{20}{80} = x\%$, or $\frac{20}{80} = \frac{1}{4} = 0.25$. Convert 0.25 to a percent by multiplying by 100 (or moving the decimal point two places to the right), and you have your answer: $0.25 = 25\%$.

TIP

Some questions ask you to find a percentage of a value and then increase or decrease that value by the percentage. You can perform each of these tasks in one step:

>> To increase a number by a particular percentage of that number, multiply the number by 1 and the percentage. So, to find the total purchase amount of a $9.50 item with 6% tax, multiply 9.50 by 1.06: $9.50 \times 1.06 = 10.07$.

>> To decrease a number by a particular percentage of that number, multiply the number by the percentage you get when you subtract the original percentage from 100. So, to find the sale price of a $9.50 item that has been discounted by 6%, multiply 9.50 by 94% (100 – 6%): $9.50 \times .94 = 8.93$.

Ratios

Here's what you need to know to answer ratio problems:

TIP

>> A *ratio* is written as $\frac{of}{to}$ or of:to. The ratio *of* sunflowers *to* roses = $\frac{\text{sunflowers}}{\text{roses}}$. The ratio *of* umbrellas *to* heads = umbrellas:heads.

When you see a ratio written with colons, rewrite it as a fraction. It's easier to evaluate ratios when they're written in fraction form because you can more easily set up proportions or see that you need to give ratios common denominators to compare them.

>> **A *possible total* is a multiple of the sum of the numbers in the ratio.** For example, you may be given a problem like this: At a party, the ratio of blondes to redheads is 4:5. Which of the following could be the total number of blondes and redheads at the party? Mega-easy. Add the numbers in the ratio: $4 + 5 = 9$. The total number of blondes must be a multiple of 9, such as 9, 18, 27, 36, and so on.

REMEMBER

>> **When a question gives you a ratio and a total and asks you to find a specific term, do the following:**

1. **Add the numbers in the ratio.**

2. **Divide that sum into the total.**

3. **Multiply that quotient by each term in the ratio.**

4. **Add the answers to double-check that their sum equals the total.**

Confused? Consider this example: Yelling at the members of his team, who had just lost 21–0, the irate coach pointed his finger at each member of the squad and called every player either a wimp or a slacker. If there were 3 wimps for every 4 slackers and every member of the 28-person squad was either a wimp or a slacker, how many wimps were there?

First, add the ratio: $3 + 4 = 7$. Divide 7 into the total number of team members: $\frac{28}{7} = 4$. Multiply 4 by each term in the ratio: $4 \times 3 = 12$; $4 \times 4 = 16$. Make sure those numbers add up to the total number of team members: $12 + 16 = 28$. Now you have all the information you need to answer a variety of questions.

The ACT may toss in a few proportion problems, too. A *proportion* is a relationship between two ratios where the ratios are equal. Just like with fractions, multiplying or dividing both numbers in the ratio by the same number doesn't change the value of the ratio. So, for example, these two ratios make up a proportion: 2:8 and 4:16, which you may also see written as $\frac{2}{8} = \frac{4}{16}$.

Often, you see a couple of equal ratios with a missing term that you have to find. To solve these problems, you *cross-multiply*. In other words, you multiply the terms that are diagonal from each other and solve for *x*. In this block, see the earlier section "Basic operations with fractions" for details about how to cross-multiply and "Elementary algebra" later on for details about solving for *x*.

Exponents

TIP

Many ACT questions require you to know how to work with bases and exponents. Exponents represent repeated multiplication. For example, 5^3 is the same as $5 \times 5 \times 5 = 125$. When you work with exponents, make sure you know these important concepts:

>> The *base* is the big value on the bottom. The *exponent* is the little value in the upper-right corner. In 5^3, 5 is the base and 3 is the exponent.

>> A base to the zero power equals one. For example, $5^0 = 1$; $x^0 = 1$.

>> When you have a negative exponent, just put the base and exponent under a 1 and make the exponent positive again. For example, $5^{-3} = \dfrac{1}{5^3}$. The resulting number is not negative. When you flip it, you get the reciprocal, and the negative just sort of fades away.

>> **You can rewrite a fractional exponent as a radical.** For example, $5^{\frac{2}{3}} = \sqrt[3]{5^2}$. See "Roots and radicals" later in this block.

>> **To multiply like bases, add the exponents.** For example, $5^4 \times 5^9 = 5^{4+9} = 5^{13}$.

You can't multiply *unlike* bases. You actually have to work out the problem.

>> **To divide like bases, subtract the exponents.** For example, $5^9 \div 5^3 = 5^{9-3} = 5^6$.

>> **Multiply the exponents of a base inside and outside the parentheses.** That's quite a mouthful. Here's what it means: $\left(5^3\right)^2 = 5^{3\times2} = 5^6$.

>> **When like bases are variables that have like exponents, you can add or subtract the numerical coefficient of the bases.** The *numerical coefficient* is simply the number in front of the base (so the 5 in 5x). The numerical coefficient of any variable on its own is 1: $x = 1x$. Here are two examples of adding and subtracting bases that are variables that have like exponents:

$$37x^3 + 10x^3 = 47x^3$$
$$15y^2 - 5y^2 = 10y^2$$

Order of operations

When you have several operations (addition, subtraction, multiplication, division, squaring, and so on) in one problem, you must perform the operations in the following order:

1. Parentheses.

Do what's inside the parentheses first.

2. Exponent.

Do the squaring or the cubing (whatever the exponent is).

3. Multiply or divide.

Do multiplication and division left to right. If multiplication is to the left of division, multiply first. If division is to the left of multiplication, divide first.

4. Add or subtract.

Do addition and subtraction left to right. If addition is to the left of subtraction, add first. If subtraction is to the left of addition, subtract first.

An easy *mnemonic* (memory device) for remembering the order of operations is *PEMDAS*: Parentheses, Exponents, Multiply, Divide, Add, Subtract.

Average, median, mode, and range

The ACT might ask you a few basic statistics questions (it contains more advanced probability and statistics problems, too, covered later in this block). Most of these questions ask about average (also known as *average mean* or just *mean*).

The *median* is the middle value in a list of several values or numbers. The *mode* is the value that occurs most often in a set of values. The *range* is the distance from the greatest to the smallest. In other words, just subtract the smallest term from the largest term to find the range.

If you need to review the average formula or how it's different from *median* and *mode*, do a Google search for **mean, median, and mode review**. You can also benefit from reviewing how weighted averages work.

You can use given values in the average formula to solve for the other values. In other words, if the exam gives you the average and the sum of a group of numbers, you can figure out how many numbers are in the set by using the average formula.

Elementary algebra

Algebra is just arithmetic in which symbols called *variables* — usually letters x, y, and z — stand in for numbers. The ACT gives you all sorts of opportunities to "solve the equation for x."

One of the first algebraic procedures you need to know is how to solve for x in an equation. Try out this procedure by solving for x in this equation: $3x + 7 = 9x - 5$.

1. Isolate the variable.

Move the $3x$ to the right by subtracting it from both sides. In other words, *change the sign* to make it $-3x$.

WARNING

Forgetting to change the sign is one of the most common careless mistakes that students make. To catch this mistake on the ACT, test makers often include trap answer choices that you'd get if you forgot to change the sign.

Move the -5 to the left, changing the sign to make it $+5$. You now have $7 + 5 = 9x - 3x$.

2. Add the x's on one side; subtract the non-x's on the other side.
$12 = 6x$

3. Divide both sides by the 6 that's next to the x.
$2 = x$

TIP

If you absolutely hate algebra, see whether you can simply plug in the answer choices. Start with the easiest number first. For example, start with 2, not $3\frac{1}{2}$.

If a question asks you to add together two or more expressions, you can set them up vertically like you would for an addition problem in arithmetic. Just remember that you can combine only like terms (for example $3x$ and $2x$, not $3x$ and $4y$) this way. Here's an example:

$$
\begin{aligned}
3x + 4y - 7z \\
2x - 2y + 8z \\
\underline{-x + 3y + 6z} \\
4x + 3y + 7z
\end{aligned}
$$

To subtract expressions, distribute the minus sign throughout the second expression and then combine the like terms. (See "Distributive property of multiplication" earlier in this block.) Here's an example of how to subtract two expressions:

$$\left(2x^2 - 3xy - 6y^2\right) - \left(-4x^2 - 6xy + 2y^2\right) = 2x^2 - 3xy - 6y^2 + 4x^2 + 6xy - 2y^2 = 6x^2 + 3xy - 8y^2 =$$

WARNING

Notice that distributing the minus sign changes the signs of all the terms in the second expression. Make sure you keep the signs straight when you subtract expressions.

When you multiply a term by a *binomial* (an expression with two terms), you have to multiply the number by each term in the binomial, like so:

$$4x(x-3) = 4x(x)-12x = 4x^2 - 12x$$

To divide a binomial, just divide each term in the binomial by the term, like so:

$$\frac{16x^2+4x}{4x} = \frac{16x^2}{4x} + \frac{4x}{4x} = 4x+1$$

When you have to multiply two binomials, use the FOIL method. *FOIL* stands for *First, Outer, Inner, Last* and refers to the order in which you multiply the variables in parentheses when you multiply two expressions.

TIP

You need to out-and-out *memorize* the following three FOIL problems. Don't bother to work them out every time; know them by heart. Doing so saves you time, careless mistakes, and acute misery on the actual exam.

» $(a+b)^2 = a^2 + 2ab + b^2$

You can prove this equation by using FOIL to multiply $(a+b)(a+b)$.

1. **Multiply the *First* terms:** $a(a)=a^2$.

2. **Multiply the *Outer* terms:** $a(-b)=-ab$.

3. **Multiply the *Inner* terms:** $b(a)=ba$.

4. **Multiply the *Last* terms:** $b(b)=b^2$.

5. **Combine like terms:** $ab+ab=2ab$.

   The final solution is $a^2 + 2ab + b^2$.

» $(a-b)^2 = a^2 - 2ab + b^2$

You can prove this equation by using FOIL to multiply $(a-b)(a-b)$.

Notice that the b^2 at the end is positive, not negative, because multiplying a negative times a negative gives you a positive.

» $(a-b)(a+b) = a^2 - b^2$

You can prove this equation by using FOIL to multiply $(a-b)(a+b)$.

Note that the middle term drops out because $+ab$ cancels out $-ab$.

Factoring

Factors are the terms that make up a product. Extracting common factors can make expressions much easier to deal with. See how many common factors you can find in this expression; then extract, or *factor*, them out:

$$-14x^3 - 35x^6$$

1. First, you can pull out –7 because it goes into both –14 and –35. Doing so gives you $-7(2x^3 + 5x^6)$.

2. Next, you can take out the common factor of x^3 because x^3 is part of both terms. The simplified result is $-7x^3(2+5x^3)$.

You also need to know how to factor quadratic equations, which you accomplish by using FOIL in reverse. Say that the test gives you $x^2 + 13x + 42 = 0$ and asks you to solve for x. Take this problem one step at a time:

1. **Draw two sets of parentheses.**

   $(\ )(\ ) = 0$

2. **To get x^2, the *First* terms have to be x and x, so fill those in first.**

   $(x\ )(x\ ) = 0$

3. **Look at the *Outer* terms.**

   You need two numbers that multiply together to get +42. Well, you have several possibilities: 42 and 1, 21 and 2, or 6 and 7. You can even have two negative numbers: –42 and –1, –21 and –2, or –6 and –7. You can't be sure which numbers to choose yet, so go on to the next step.

4. **Look at the *Inner* terms.**

   You have to add two values to get +13. What's the first thing that springs to mind? Probably 6 + 7. Hey, that's one of the possible combinations of numbers you came up with in Step 3 for the *Outer* terms! Plug them in and multiply.

   $$(x+6)(x+7) =$$
   $$x^2 + 7x + 6x + 42 =$$
   $$x^2 + 13x + 42 =$$

5. **Solve for x.**

   If the whole equation equals 0, then either $(x+6) = 0$ or $(x+7) = 0$. After all, any number times 0 equals 0. Therefore, when you solve for x for either of these possibilities, x can equal –6 or –7.

TIP

Whenever you see an ACT problem that includes a quadratic equation, you can pretty much bet you're going to have to perform some factoring. Make sure you're familiar with the steps because factoring problems crop up frequently. Or you can use your graphing calculator to factor quadratic equations. If your calculator doesn't already contain the program, you can find ways to add the program on the Internet.

Solving a system of equations

Suppose you have two algebraic equations with two different variables. For example, an ACT question may ask you to solve for x when $4x + 5y = 30$ and $y + x = 2$. You're dealing with a *system of equations*. By themselves, there could be an infinite number of values for x and y. However, when considered together, there is only one value for x and one value for y as long as the two equations aren't equal.

There are two ways to solve for a variable in simultaneous equations: substitution or elimination. Here, we show you elimination because it may be easier, especially when you're working with more complex equations. Basically, you stack the equations and manipulate them so you can eliminate one variable and solve for the other.

Here's how it's done for this problem. To get rid of the y variable, change y in the second equation to $-5y$. You can accomplish this feat by multiplying every term in the second equation by -5: $(-5)y + (-5)x = (-5)2$. It's legal to change the equation as long as you perform the same operation with each of its terms, as explained earlier in "Elementary algebra." The resulting equation is $-5y - 5x = -10$. Just change the order of the first equation so the like terms match up, stack the two equations, and solve for x:

$$5y + 4x = 30$$
$$\underline{-5y - 5x = -10}$$
$$0 - x = 20$$
$$x = -20$$

If an ACT question tells you that a system of linear equations has no solutions, create equal equations. The ACT may give you the following equations, tell you that there are unlimited solutions for the system, and ask you to solve for a.

$$5y + 4x = 30$$
$$-15y - 12x = -10a$$

You just need to recognize that the second equation is the same as the first with each term multiplied by -3. Therefore, the value for a that would make the third term equal to 30×-3 is 9: $30 \times -3 = -10(9)$.

So don't get discouraged if you see two equations with two similar variables. You have several tools for dealing with them. They're not as hard to work with as you think!

Reviewing geometry and trig

Geometry may seem like one of the areas that can mess you up on the ACT. But it's easy when you take the time to memorize some rules. This section provides a lightning-fast review of the major points of geometry so that you can go into the test equipped to tackle the geometry questions with ease.

Types of lines

Here are the common terms about lines that you should know (or look up) before you take the ACT: *line segment, midpoint, intersect, vertical, horizontal, parallel,* and *perpendicular.*

Types of angles

Angle problems make up a big part of the ACT geometry test. Fortunately, understanding angles is easy when you memorize a few basic concepts. After all, you don't have to do any proofs on the test. Finding an angle is usually a matter of simple addition or subtraction.

To succeed on the ACT, you need to know the following things about angles:

>> **Acute angles** are greater than 0 but less than 90 degrees. Think of an acute angle as being a *cute* little angle.

>> **Right angles** are equal to 90 degrees. They're formed by perpendicular lines and indicated by a box in the corner of the two intersecting lines.

>> **Obtuse angles** that are greater than 90 degrees but less than 180 degrees. Think of an obtuse angle as obese (or fat) angle.

>> **Straight angles** measure exactly 180 degrees.

>> **Complementary angles** total 90 degrees. Think of C for the 90 degree corner.

>> **Supplementary angles** total 180 degrees. If you're likely to confuse complementary and supplementary angles, think alphabetically: *C* comes before *S* in the alphabet; 90 comes before 180 when you count.

>> **Reflex angles** are greater than 180 degrees but less than 360 degrees.

>> **Angles around a point** total 360 degrees.

>> **Exterior angles** of any figure are supplementary to the two opposite interior angles and always total 360 degrees.

>> **Vertical angles** are opposite each other and have equal measures. Weirdly, they don't have to be vertical; they can be horizontal too.

>> **Corresponding angles** are in the same position around two parallel lines and a transversal. When you see these, number the angles as shown in Figure 2-2. Then all odd-numbered angles are equal and all even-numbered angles are equal

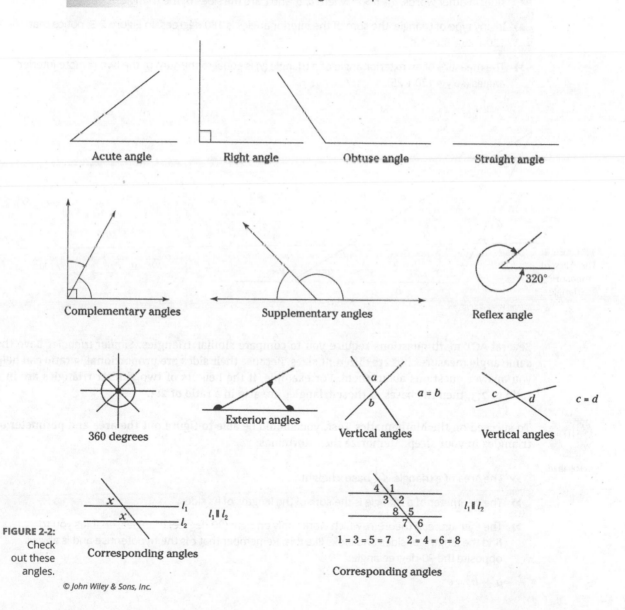

Acute angle   Right angle   Obtuse angle   Straight angle

Complementary angles   Supplementary angles   Reflex angle
320°

360 degrees   Exterior angles   Vertical angles   Vertical angles
$a = b$ $c = d$

x l_1
x l_2 $l_1 \parallel l_2$ Corresponding angles

$4 \backslash 1$
$3 \backslash 2$
$8 \backslash 5$ $l_1 \parallel l_2$
$7 \backslash 6$

$1 = 3 = 5 = 7$ $2 = 4 = 6 = 8$

Corresponding angles

FIGURE 2-2:
Check out these angles.

© John Wiley & Sons, Inc.

Triangles

Many of the geometry problems on the ACT require you to know a lot about triangles. Remember the facts and rules about triangles in this section, and you're on your way to acing geometry questions.

Triangles are classified based on the measurements of their sides and angles. Here are the types of triangles you may need to know for the ACT: equilateral, isosceles, and scalene.

When you're figuring out ACT questions that deal with triangles, you need to know these rules about the measurements of their sides and angles. Figure 2-3 illustrates these rules:

>> In any triangle, the largest angle (120 degrees in Figure 2-3) is opposite the longest side (c).

>> In any triangle, the sum of the lengths of two sides must be greater than the length of the third side. In other words, $a + b > c$, where a, b, and c are the sides of the triangle.

>> In any type of triangle, the sum of the interior angles is 180 degrees. In Figure 2-3, notice that $120 + 25 + 35 = 180$.

>> The measure of an exterior angle of a triangle (y) is equal to the sum of the two remote interior angles (so $y = 120 + 25$).

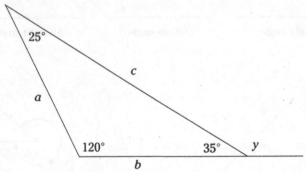

FIGURE 2-3:
The rules of measuring triangles.

© John Wiley & Sons, Inc.

Several ACT math questions require you to compare similar triangles. *Similar triangles* have the same angle measures but are different sizes. Because their sides are proportional, a ratio can help you answer questions about them. For example, if the heights of two similar triangles are in a ratio of 2:3, then the bases of those triangles are also in a ratio of 2:3.

REMEMBER

To succeed on the Mathematics Test, you should be able to figure out the area and perimeter of triangles in your sleep. Memorize these formulas:

>> The area of a triangle is $\frac{1}{2}$ base × height.

>> The perimeter of a triangle is the sum of the lengths of its sides.

>> The Pythagorean theorem, which works only on right (90-degree) triangles, enables you to find the lengths of sides and looks like this. Remember that c is the hypotenuse and is always opposite the 90-degree angle:

$$a^2 + b^2 = c^2$$

Quadrilaterals

Another favorite figure of the ACT test-making folks is the *quadrilateral*, which is the fancy label mathematicians give shapes with four sides. For the ACT, here's what you need to know about quadrilaterals:

>> The interior angles of any quadrilateral total 360 degrees. So, you can cut any quadrilateral into two 180-degree triangles. Knowing this can help you find the area of strange quadrilateral shapes.

>> Know the properties and how to find the area of the following types of quadrilaterals: square, rhombus, rectangle, parallelogram, trapezoid.

TIP

Knowing how to find the area of quadrilaterals (those with both neat and strange shapes) and other figures can help you solve *shaded-area* or *leftover* problems, in which you have to subtract the unshaded area from the total area.

Polygons

Triangles and quadrilaterals are probably the most commonly tested polygons on the ACT. What's a polygon? A *polygon* is a closed-plane figure bounded by straight sides.

Here's what you need to know about the side and angle measurements of polygons:

>> A *regular* polygon, such as a square, has all equal sides and all equal angles.

The ACT rarely asks you to find the areas of any polygons with more than four sides.

>> The *perimeter* of a polygon is the sum of the lengths of all the sides.

>> The *exterior angle measure* of any polygon, also known as the sum of its exterior angles, is 360 degrees. (An *exterior angle* is the angle formed by any side of the polygon and the line that's created when you extend the adjacent side.)

>> To find the *interior angle measure* of any regular polygon, also known as the sum of its interior angles, use the formula $(n-2)180°$, where n stands for the number of sides. For example, to find the interior angle measure for a pentagon (a five-sided figure), just substitute 5 for n in the formula and solve:

$$(5-2)180° = 3 \times 180 = 540°$$

So the sum of the interior angles of a pentagon is 540°.

REMEMBER

The volume of any polygon is area of the base × height.

Circles

Did you hear about the rube who pulled his son out of college, claiming that the school was filling his head with nonsense? As the rube said, "Joe Bob told me that he learned πr^2. But any fool knows that *pie* are round; *cornbread* are square!"

Circles are among the least complicated geometry concepts. To excel on circle questions, you must be able to recognize and know the properties of the following elements of a circle, most of which are shown in Figure 2-4: radius (r), midpoint (M), diameter (d), chord (d and c), central angle (ABC), inscribed angle (XYZ), arc, sector, and tangent line.

FIGURE 2-4:
Some
elements
of a circle.

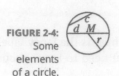
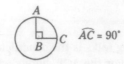
Central angle
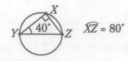
Inscribed angle

$\overparen{AC} = 90°$

$\overparen{XZ} = 80°$

When you know the preceding terms, you can use the following concepts to help you answers questions about circles:

>> The area of a circle is πr^2, where r is the radius.

>> The circumference of a circle is $2\pi r$ or πd because two radii equal one diameter.

On the Math Test, if you're asked how much distance a wheel covers or how many times a clock hand revolves, know that one rotation of a wheel or minute hand equals one circumference of that wheel or clock.

>> The degree measure of a circle is 360.

>> The degree measure of a central angle is the same as the degree measure of its intercepted arc.

>> The degree measure of an inscribed angle is half the degree measure of its intercepted arc. This information is helpful if you're familiar with Thales's theorem.

>> When a central angle and an inscribed angle have the same endpoints, the degree measure of the central angle is twice that of the inscribed angle.

>> The degree measure of an arc is the same as its central angle and twice its inscribed angle.

>> The degree measure of a sector is the same as its central angle and twice its inscribed angle.

>> A tangent line is always perpendicular to the radius at the point on the circumference where the line touches the circle.

>> A pair of lines drawn from an external point and both tangent to different points on the circumference of a circle are congruent.

The ACT may also ask you to find the length of an arc or find the area of a sector.

Trigonometry

Many of our students cringe when they hear that the ACT has trigonometry questions. If you're cringing right now, too, relax and stand tall. The ACT has only a few trig questions, and this section covers what you need to know to answer most of those few, even if you've never stepped foot in a trigonometry classroom.

Dealing with trigonometric functions is about all you need to know for most of the trig questions. *Trigonometric functions* express the relationships between the angles and sides of a right triangle in terms of one of its angles. You can answer almost every ACT trig question if you remember the mnemonic for the three basic trigonometric functions, SOH CAH TOA.

SOH CAH TOA stands for

$$\text{Sine} = \frac{\text{opposite}}{\text{hypotenuse}}$$

$$\text{Cosine} = \frac{\text{adjacent}}{\text{hypotenuse}}$$

$$\text{Tangent} = \frac{\text{opposite}}{\text{adjacent}}$$

Are you scratching your head now and asking, "Opposite? Opposite *what?*" Take a look at this right triangle and consider the guidelines that follow it.

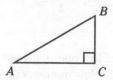

Side *AB* is the *hypotenuse* of the triangle. In relation to the angle at point *A*, side *BC* is the *opposite* side. The other side, the one that's not the hypotenuse or opposite angle *A*, is the *adjacent* side. When you know how to decode these trigonometric functions, you can mostly plug and chug and answers questions about triangles. If you need to see this trigonometry in action first, check out the sample questions in Block 3, the practice test answers in Block 4, or the Numberphile channel on YouTube (www.youtube.com/@numberphile).

Solving algebraic equations and more

The ACT tests your knowledge of core high school subjects, and most high schools require students to study algebra. For the basics of algebra, see "Elementary algebra" earlier in this block. This section reviews more advanced algebra concepts, including dealing with inequalities, radicals, functions, and even logarithms. We also outline what you need to know to work with questions that cover the coordinate plane.

Inequalities

Mathematical expressions don't always involve equal sides. On the ACT, you'll see a few symbols of inequality. Table 2-1 shows the more commonly used algebra symbols that signify inequality.

TABLE 2-1 Mathematical Symbols for Inequality

Symbol	Meaning
≠	Not equal to
>	Greater than
<	Less than
≥	Greater than or equal to
≤	Less than or equal to

When you use the greater than or less than symbols, always position the wide side of the arrow toward the bigger value, like so: $5 > 2$ or $2 < 5$.

You can solve for *x* in simple inequalities the same way you do in equations. Just add or subtract the same number to or from both sides of the inequality, and multiply or divide both sides by the same number. Here's an example:

$$x + 6 \leq 0$$
$$x \leq -6$$

REMEMBER

When you multiply or divide both sides of an inequality by a negative number, you have to reverse the direction of the inequality symbol. For example, when you simplify $-2x < 6$ by dividing both sides by -2 to isolate x, you must switch the symbol so that the final answer is $x > -3$:

$$-2x < 6$$
$$x > -3$$

You can also use inequalities to show a range of numbers instead of just one single value. To show the range of -3 to $+2$ including -3 and $+2$, use the $\leq$ sign: $-3 \leq x \leq 2$. Now numbers represented by x include -3 and 2 in the possibilities.

Complex numbers

Imaginary numbers (expressed by the variable i) are downright difficult to imagine. In fact, they don't appear on a traditional number line. The fundamental concept to remember is that i represents the value that, when squared, results in -1 ($i^2 = -1$). Besides that mind-blowing equation, here are the other rules regarding imaginary numbers that you need to know for the ACT:

>> $i = \sqrt{-1}$: If $i^2 = -1$, it stands to reason that $i = \sqrt{-1}$.

>> There are only four possible results for taking i to a power: $\sqrt{-1}$, -1, $-\sqrt{-1}$, and 1. $i^1 = \sqrt{-1}$, $i^2 = -1$, $i^3 = -\sqrt{-1}$, $i^4 = 1$. Then it repeats: $i^5 = \sqrt{-1}$, $i^6 = -1$, and so on.

>> To add imaginary numbers, just add them as you would any other variable:
$$(3i - 4) + (5i - 6) = 8i - 10$$

>> When you multiply imaginary numbers, replace i^2 with -1:

$$
\begin{aligned}
(3i - 4)(5i - 6) &= \\
15i^2 - 18i - 20i + 24 &= \\
15i^2 - 38i + 24 &= \\
15(-1) - 38i + 24 &= \\
-15 - 38i + 24 &= \\
-38i + 9 &=
\end{aligned}
$$

>> Eliminate an imaginary number in the denominator:

- For one complex term, multiply both the numerator and denominator by that term:

$$
\begin{aligned}
\frac{(3i - 4)}{5i} &= \\
\frac{(3i - 4)}{5i} \times \frac{5i}{5i} &= \\
\frac{-15i^2 - 20i}{25i^2} &= \\
\frac{15 - 20i}{-25} &=
\end{aligned}
$$

- For complex binomial terms, multiply both the numerator and denominator by the conjugate:

$$
\begin{aligned}
\frac{(3i - 4)}{(5i - 6)} &= \\
\frac{(3i - 4)}{(5i - 6)} \times \frac{(5i + 6)}{(5i + 6)} &= \\
\frac{-38i + 9}{25i^2 + 30i - 30i - 36} &= \\
\frac{-38i + 9}{25(-1) - 36} &= \\
\frac{-38i + 9}{-61} &=
\end{aligned}
$$

Roots and radicals

ACT math questions require you to know how to work with roots and radicals. For the purposes of the ACT, the two terms mean the same thing. The *square root* of a value is the number you multiply by itself to get that value. In other words, the square root of 9 (or $\sqrt{9}$) is 3 because you multiply 3 by itself to get 9. A *cube root* of a value is the number you multiply by itself 3 times to get that value. So the cube root of 27 (or $\sqrt[3]{27}$) is 3 because $3 \times 3 \times 3 = 3^3 = 27$. To simplify working with square roots or cube roots (or any other roots), think of them as variables. You work with them the same way you work with x, y, or z.

Adding and subtracting radicals is easy to do as long as you remember a couple of guidelines:

>> **To add or subtract like radicals, add or subtract the number in front of the radical.**

$$2\sqrt{7} + 5\sqrt{7} = 7\sqrt{7}$$
$$9\sqrt{13} - 4\sqrt{13} = 5\sqrt{13}$$

>> **You *can't* add or subtract unlike radicals.** For example, you can't add the following terms and get $10\sqrt{8}$.

$$6\sqrt{5} + 4\sqrt{3} = 6\sqrt{5} + 4\sqrt{3}$$

REMEMBER

When you see unlike radicals, you may be able to simplify one radical to make it match the radical in the other term. For example,

$$\sqrt{52} + \sqrt{13} = ?$$

Begin by simplifying. Take out a perfect square from the term:

$$\sqrt{52} = \sqrt{4} \times \sqrt{13}$$

Because $\sqrt{4} = 2$, $\sqrt{52} = 2\sqrt{13}$.

So you can add the two original terms:

$$\sqrt{52} + \sqrt{13} = 2\sqrt{13} + \sqrt{13} = 3\sqrt{13}$$

When you multiply or divide radicals, the motto is "just do it." All you do is multiply or divide the numbers and then pop the radical sign back onto the finished product. For example,

$$\sqrt{5} \times \sqrt{6} = \sqrt{30}$$
$$\sqrt{15} \div \sqrt{5} = \sqrt{3}$$

If you have numbers in front of the radical, multiply them as well. Let everyone in on the fun. For example,

$$6\sqrt{3} \times 4\sqrt{2} = (6 \times 4)(\sqrt{3} \times \sqrt{2}) = 24\sqrt{6}$$

REMEMBER

Whenever your calculations result in a fraction with a square root in the denominator, you have to multiply both the top and the bottom by the square root in the denominator:

$$\frac{1}{\sqrt{2}} \times \frac{\sqrt{2}}{\sqrt{2}} = \frac{\sqrt{2}}{2}$$

When you see an operation inside the radical, do it first and then take the square root. For the following example, first solve the equation inside the radical using the common denominator of 360:

$$\sqrt{\dfrac{\frac{x^2}{40}+\frac{x^2}{9}}{\sqrt{\frac{9x^2}{360}+\frac{40x^2}{360}}}}$$

$$\sqrt{\dfrac{\frac{9x^2}{360}+\frac{40x^2}{360}}{\sqrt{\frac{49x^2}{360}}}}$$

Now take the square roots of both the numerator and denominator: $\sqrt{49x^2}=7x$ (because $7x \times 7x = 49x^2$) and $\sqrt{360} \approx 18.97$. Did you say that $\sqrt{360}=6$? Nope! $\sqrt{36}=6$, but $\sqrt{360} \approx 18.97$. Beware of assuming too much; doing so may lead you down the path to temptation.

Your final answer is $\dfrac{7x}{18.97}$.

Coordinate planes

Quite a few questions on the ACT cover coordinate geometry, which involves working with points on a graph called a *Cartesian coordinate plane*. This perfectly flat surface has a system that allows you to identify the position of points by using a pair of numbers.

To answer the ACT's coordinate geometry questions, you must know how to identify the following elements on a coordinate plane: x-axis, y-axis, origin, quadrant, and ordered pairs such as the location of (2,3) or (−4, 5).

When working with elements on the coordinate plane, keep these rules in mind:

>> A line connecting points with the same *x*- and *y*-coordinates — (1, 1), (2, 2), and (3, 3), for example — forms a 45-degree angle (see Figure 2-5).

>> To locate the middle point of a line, use the *midpoint formula*:

$$M = \left(\frac{x_1 + x_2}{2}, \frac{y_1 + y_2}{2} \right)$$

>> To find the distance between two points, use the *distance formula*:

$$\sqrt{\left(x_2 - x_1\right)^2 + \left(y_2 - y_1\right)^2}$$

>> *Slope* measures how steep a line is. It's commonly referred to as *rise over run*. Think of slope as a fraction. A slope of 4 is really a slope of $\frac{4}{1}$. One way to find the slope of a line is to locate two of its points and apply the formula for slope:

$$Slope = \frac{y_2 - y_1}{x_2 - x_1}$$

>> The *equation of a line* (or slope-intercept form) is $y = mx + b$. The *m* is the slope of the line, and the *b* is where the line crosses the y-axis (called the y-intercept). So a line with an equation of $y = 4x + 1$ has a slope of $\frac{4}{1}$ and a y-intercept of 1.

FIGURE 2-5:
A line
connecting
points with
the same
x- and y-
coordinates.

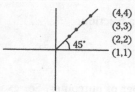

(4,4)
(3,3)
(2,2)
45°
(1,1)

© John Wiley & Sons, Inc.

Functions

If you've never studied functions, don't worry. The ACT doesn't ask you a lot of function questions. And the ones that do appear are relatively easy. You're essentially just applying substitution. For example, you may see a problem like this one:

$$f(x) = (2x)^2$$

Solve for $f(2)$.

The function shows the relationship between x and y. $f(x) = y$, and x is the x-coordinate you plug into the function to solve for y. So, the $f(2)$ supplies the x-value (2) you input into the function. The output is the y-value that results when you input the 2 into the function and solve. In other words, just plug in the 2 where you see an x in the equation to find the corresponding value for y, or $f(x)$:

$$f(2) = (2 \times 2)^2 = 4^2 = 16$$

You may also need to find functions of variables. Treat them exactly the same way that you do actual values. So if you're given $f(x) = (2x)^2$ and asked to find $f(x+y)$, you solve by following the same steps:

1. **Substitute all the stuff in the parentheses (x + y) for x in the original function:**

$$f(x+y) = [2(x+y)]^2$$

2. **Distribute the 2:**

$$f(x+y) = (2x+2y)^2$$

3. **Square the binomial expression:**

$$f(x+y) = (2x+2y)(2x+2y)$$
$$f(x+y) = 4x^2 + 4xy + 4xy + 4y^2$$
$$f(x+y) = 4x^2 + 8xy + 4y^2$$

Regardless of what's inside the parentheses of the function, you substitute that for x in the original function.

Probability

Probability questions are usually word problems. They may look intimidating, with so many words that make you lose sight of where to begin, but they aren't impossible to solve.

TIP

No matter what kind of probability problems you face, remember that probability can only be 0, 1, or a number in between 0 and 1. You can't have a negative probability, and you can't have a probability greater than 1, or 100 percent.

To find a probability of one event, use this formula to set up a fraction:

$$P = \frac{\text{Number of possible desired outcomes}}{\text{Number of total possible outcomes}}$$

Start by identifying the denominator, or total possible number of outcomes. For example, when you're flipping a coin, the denominator of 2. When you're pulling a card from a full deck, the denominator is 52.

Next, find your numerator. If you're flipping a coin, you have one chance of getting heads. If you want to draw a jack from the deck of cards, you have four chances. Therefore, your chance of tossing heads is $\frac{1}{2}$ and the probability of drawing a jack out of a deck of cards is $\frac{4}{52}$ (which reduces to $\frac{1}{13}$).

You can find the probability of multiple events by following several rules. Table 2-2 lists and describes each rule, shows the corresponding formula, and provides an example of when you'd use it.

TABLE 2-2 Finding the Probability of the Occurrence of Multiple Events

Rule	Circumstance	Formula	Example
Special Rule of Addition	The probability of the occurrence of either of two possible events that are mutually exclusive	$P(A \text{ or } B) = P(A) + P(B)$	The probability of rolling a 5 or 6 on one roll of one die
General Rule of Addition	The probability of the occurrence of either of two possible events that can happen together	$P(A \text{ or } B) = P(A) + P(B) - P(A \text{ and } B)$	The probability of drawing a playing card that displays a club or a queen
Special Rule of Multiplication	The probability of the occurrence of two events at the same time when the two events are independent of each other	$P(A \text{ and } B) = P(A) \times P(B)$	The probability of rolling a 5 and a 6 on one roll of two dice
General Rule of Multiplication	The probability of the occurrence of two events when the occurrence of the first event affects the outcome of the second event	$P(A \text{ and } B) = P(A) \times P(B/A)$ (The line between the B and A stands for "B given A"; it doesn't mean divide.)	The probability of first drawing the queen of clubs from a pack of 52 cards, keeping the queen of clubs out of the pack, and then drawing the jack of diamonds on the next try

Calculating outcomes and orderings

A few questions in each Mathematics Test will ask for the possible number of outcomes, either combinations or orderings for particular events. Some of these problems are easy; others may require you to dust off the chapter on factorials from math textbooks past.

COMBINATIONS

When a question asks for the total possible outcomes given two or more events and order isn't an issue, you're dealing with a *combination*. Apply the counting principle. The counting principle just means that you multiply the number of possibilities for one event by the number of possibilities for the other event. Say you go to an ice cream social that offers three flavors of ice cream, five kinds of toppings, and four different-patterned bowls to put them in. To determine the number of different combinations you could pick for one ice cream flavor, one topping, and one bowl, you just multiply $3 \times 4 \times 5$. That's 60 different combinations to choose from!

Calculations become a little more complex when you must create combinations with a smaller number of members than the original pool. For example, say you want to know how many possible five-number lock combinations you can create from the ten possible 1-digit numbers when the order of the lock combination doesn't matter and no number is repeated. Here's where factorials come into the picture.

The *factorial function* designates the product of descending whole numbers. Its symbol is the exclamation point, !. So $4! = 4 \times 3 \times 2 \times 1$. The formula for finding the number of possible combinations of fewer elements drawn from a greater pool is this:

$$\frac{n!}{r!(n-r)!}$$

The n signifies the total number options to draw from, and the r stands for the number in the groups you're putting together.

So for the lock scenario, you set up the formula like this:

$$\frac{10!}{5!(10-5)!}$$

In the formula, n is 10 because there are ten digits to choose from (0, 1, 2, 3, 4, 5, 6, 7, 8, 9); r is 5 because you seek to create five-number combinations from the ten total digits.

To calculate the number of combinations, expand the formula:

$$\frac{10 \times 9 \times 8 \times 7 \times 6 \times 5 \times 4 \times 3 \times 2 \times 1}{5 \times 4 \times 3 \times 2 \times 1(5!)} = C$$

The $5 \times 4 \times 3 \times 2 \times 1$ in the numerator and denominator cancel to give you this:

$$\frac{10 \times 9 \times 8 \times 7 \times 6}{(5)!} = C$$

You can then calculate the answer like this:

$$\frac{10 \times 9 \times 8 \times 7 \times 6}{(5)!} = C$$

$$\frac{10 \times 9 \times 8 \times 7 \times 6}{5 \times 4 \times 3 \times 2 \times 1} = C$$

$$\frac{30,240}{120} = C$$

$$252 = C$$

There are 252 possible five-number lock combinations from all ten digits when order doesn't matter and no digits are repeated.

PERMUTATIONS

Permutations problems ask you to determine how many arrangements of numbers are possible given a specific set of numbers and a particular order for the arrangements. For example, figuring out the number of possible seven-digit telephone numbers you can create is a permutation problem. And the answer is huge (10^7) because you have ten possible values (the integers between 0 and 9) to fill each of the seven places.

REMEMBER

Order matters when you set up permutations. Two different phone numbers may have the same combination of numbers, such as 345-7872 and 543-7728, but the numbers ring two different phones because you input them in a different order. Rely on factorials to figure out permutations.

Suppose a photographer wants to know how many different ways she can arrange five people in a single row for a wedding photo. The number of possible arrangements of the five-person wedding party is 5! or $5! = 5 \times 4 \times 3 \times 2 \times 1 = 120$.

As you can see, more possible arrangements exist as the number of objects in the arrangement increases.

Permutations get a little more challenging when you have a fixed number of objects, *n*, to fill a limited number of places, *r*, and you care about the order the objects are arranged in.

For example, consider the predicament of the big-league baseball coach of a 20-member team who needs to determine the number of different batting orders that these 20 ball players can fill in a nine-slot batting lineup. The coach could work this permutation out by writing all the factors from 20 back nine places (because 20 players can fill only nine slots in the batting order), like this:

$$20 \times 19 \times 18 \times 17 \times 16 \times 15 \times 14 \times 13 \times 12 = x$$

But this time-consuming process isn't practical in the middle of a game. Luckily, the coach can rely on the permutation formula for *n* objects taken *r*:

$$_nP_r = \frac{n!}{(n-r)!}$$

Apply the formula to figure out the possible number of batting orders:

$$_nP_r = \frac{n!}{(n-r)!}$$

$$_nP_r = \frac{20!}{(20-9)!}$$

$$_nP_r = \frac{20!}{11!}$$

That's all there is to it. Now you can apply the outcome formulas to a sample problem.

Sequences

A sequence is a set of ordered values. Every ACT Math Test is likely to contain at least one question that deals with sequences. Commonly tested sequences on the ACT can be one of two kinds:

>> **Arithmetic sequences are formed by adding a common value (called the common difference) to each term.** The following sequence has a common difference of 3: {0, 3, 6, 9}. This sequence has a common difference of –2: {8, 6, 4, 2, 0}. Both sequences are formed by adding the common difference to one term to get the next term.

>> **Geometric sequences are formed by multiplying each term by a common value (called the common ratio).** This geometric sequence has a common ratio of 3: {3, 9, 27, 81}. A geometric sequence with a common ratio of $\frac{1}{3}$ could look like this: {81, 27, 9, 3}.

ACT math questions may ask you to find specific terms in or the sum of a sequence of values. To answer these questions, keep in mind some important rules:

>> **To find the *n*th term of an arithmetic sequence,** apply the following rule, where *n* represents the position of the term in the sequence, a_1 is the first term, and *d* is the common difference between the terms.

$$a_n = a_1 + d(n-1)$$

>> **To find the *n*th term of a geometric sequence,** apply the following rule, where *n* represents the position of the term in the sequence, a_1 is the first term, and *r* is the common ratio.

$$a_n = a_1 r^{(n-1)}$$

>> **To find the sum of a sequence of numbers,** apply the following rule, where *n* represents the number of terms in the sequence, a_1 is the first term, and *d* is the common difference between the terms.

$$Sum = \frac{n}{2}[2a_1 + d(n-1)]$$

You can bet that the answer choices will include $\frac{7x}{6}$.

Other algebra questions you might see

If you feel confident all the math covered earlier in this block and just can't get enough math preparation before you take the ACT, the following topics are other math questions that might come up. If you have time, use Khan Academy, Numberphile, or your favorite math-review resource to polish your skills in the following:

>> **Percent increase:** This type of question might ask you what percent increase or decrease occurred in the number of games a team won or the amount of commission a person earned.

>> **Logarithms:** These are essentially the number of times you multiply the base times itself to get the big number. You might see questions that ask you to apply logarithm rules or that ask about a natural logarithm.

>> **Advanced coordinate plane questions:** For these, you need to know about graphing a linear inequality, a quadratic equation, a parabola, a circle, an ellipse, and a hyperbola. You may also be asked about evaluating graphs of functions.

>> **Matrices:** A matrix is simply an array of values. Although you can perform several operations with matrices, the ACT will likely ask you to multiply them.

Comprehending the Reading Test

The Reading Test consists of four passages, each with 10 questions, for a total of 40 questions. Each passage is supposed to be similar in difficulty to materials you encounter during your freshman year of college. In this section, you find out what types of passages to expect and what the questions look like.

Understanding the topics

The test contains one passage on each of the following topics:

>> **Literary narrative:** The first passage in the section is a fiction passage from a novel or a short story. Some of the fiction passages are very fun to read. But don't expect that you'll have read them before.

>> **Social studies:** The social studies passage covers sociology, anthropology, history, geography, psychology, political science, and economics. That's an incredibly wide range of topics when you think about it. The history passages are generally easier to understand; some of the psychology ones can be intense.

>> **Humanities:** The third passage can be about music, dance, theater, art, architecture, language, ethics, literary criticism, and even philosophy. Most students tend to like the humanities passages because (believe it or not) they're actually interesting.

>> **Natural sciences:** The last passage is what most people think about when they hear the word *science*. The natural sciences passage can cover chemistry, biology, physics, and other physical sciences. If you haven't studied the subject covered, don't worry. Everything you need to answer the questions is in the passage.

Identifying the question types

The ACT Reading Test presents a variety of question types, but don't get too hung up on question types. Generally, you're simply examining the passage until it tells you the answers. Although you may encounter many different types of reading questions on the ACT, most fall into one of the following general types:

>> *Big picture questions* ask you about the passage as a whole.

>> *Detail questions* ask you to regurgitate information straight from the passage.

>> *Inference questions* require you to make logical assumptions about the passage details.

The next sections break down each of these question types and explain how to answer them correctly.

Analyze big-picture ideas or details

Questions that ask you for key point or details require a careful examination of the passage and its paragraphs.

Big picture questions are almost always the first questions in the set of ten questions for a passage. A question may ask, "Which of the following is the main idea of the passage?" or "The primary purpose of Paragraph 3 is to do which of these?" You've likely tackled big picture questions like these on other exams. As you answer them on the ACT, keep in mind these three characteristics of the overall idea:

>> **The big picture is broad and general.** It covers the entire passage (or the entire paragraph, if the question asks about a paragraph). Avoid choosing an answer that's true but focuses on a minor detail. The mere fact that a statement is true doesn't mean it's the main idea.

>> **The answer to a big picture question may repeat the topic sentence or key words.** If the passage is about Asian philosophy, the correct answer may have the words *Asian philosophy*

in it. Don't immediately choose any answer just because it has those words, but if you're debating between two answers, the one with the key words may be the better choice.

>> **The answer to a big picture question is always consistent with the tone of the passage and the attitude of the author.** If the passage is positive and the author is impressed by the philosophy, the main idea will be positive, not negative or neutral. If the author is criticizing something, the main idea will be negative.

The *detail question* covers one particular point, not the passage as a whole. Use word clues from the wording of the question or its answer choices to determine where to go in the passage to find the information that will fairly obviously give you the specific answer.

TIP

The ACT often provides clues that you're dealing with a detail question with answers directly stated in the passage. Questions that ask for information "according to the passage" or for what the author or passage *states*, *claims*, *indicates*, and so on, usually offer up answer choices that are word-for-word copies or really obvious paraphrases of information directly stated in the passage. Some sample questions include "According to the passage, James confronted Gary about the business when which of the following occurred?"

If you read actively by noting the main point of each paragraph, as explained in Block 1, your notes can help you find details in a passage quickly.

Determine craft and structure

Some questions ask you to evaluate word meanings, passage structure, and various points of view. Like all other questions in the reading test, look for obvious clues to the right (and wrong) answers within the language of the passage. Here are the different craft and structure questions:

>> **Vocabulary in context:** You may have to determine the meaning of a word by its use in context. These questions give you a word or phrase (usually italicized or in quotations) and its line reference and ask you for another word that provides the same meaning given what's going on in the passage. The key to finding the best answer for a vocabulary-in-context question is to substitute the answer choices for the existing word in the passage.

>> **Passage-structure questions:** You examine the flow of information in the passage and how the author develops the main point. Answer options for these questions often contain two parts. Make sure you consider the entire answer choice as you move through the four options and eliminate any answer that is only half right.

>> **Point-of-view questions:** You analyze various perspectives provided in passages. If a questions ask whether the passage is told by a first person narrator or an omniscient third person point of view, the pronouns usually reveal the answer. In the set of comparative passages, you're frequently asked to compare and contrast different perspectives on a similar topic. Read the opinions carefully to note which points people agree on and which points sets them on opposite sides. For more on comparative passages, see "nnnnnn" later in this block.

Integrate knowledge and ideas

Questions that ask you to synthesize the points and details of the passage may require you to determine an author's implications. These questions may be worded in slightly different ways, but essentially they ask you to make inferences and examine intended meanings. They may even have you examine a graph or table.

» **Inference questions:** These ask you about information that a passage implies rather than states directly. Specifically, they test your ability to draw conclusions from the information that's actually in the passage. You may have to read between the lines a little to find the answers to these questions. Look for the choice that extends the information in the passage *just a little bit.* For instance, suppose you read a passage about hummingbirds. Information in one paragraph may state that hummingbirds fly south for the winter. Information in another paragraph may say that the Speckled Rufus is a kind of hummingbird. From this information, you can infer that the Speckled Rufus flies south in the winter.

» **Most nearly means:** Occasionally, you see an ACT reading question worded this way: "When the author says that Gary was 'cleverly incommunicative,' she most nearly means that his response is which of these?" You might answer such a question easily by examining the possible answer choices. Usually the correct answer provides a definition or description of the quoted material and doesn't require you to check out the passage at all. For example, the answer to the question about Gary's response could be "Gary wisely chooses to refrain from responding to Jack's confrontation."

» **Graphs, tables, and figures:** In 2021, the ACT announced that it may start including a graph or table in the reading passages. Passages with graphs or tables and questions regarding them have appeared infrequently, however. If you encounter them, answer questions about these data points in the same way you'd approach science test data questions, explained later in this block.

Approaching comparative passages

One topic in the Reading Test will consist of two passages on the same general topic. The questions are grouped into three categories: those about the first passage, those about the second one, and those about both of them. Answer questions about the individual passages the same way you do the one-passage format. The last several questions require you to compare two passages, asking you how they're different, on which points they agree, or how one author would respond to the opinion of the other author. The trick to answering the comparison questions is to eliminate answer choices based on one passage at a time. See Block 1 for answer-elimination strategies.

Peering into the Science Test

On the ACT Science Test (which aptly enough used to be called *Science Reasoning*), you demonstrate that you have an important collegiate skill: the ability to approach novel information, sort it out, and draw conclusions from it. In other words, you don't have to know what a scientist knows, but you do need to be able to think as a scientist thinks.

The fastest way to improve your science score is by repeating this mantra to yourself as you make your way through the test: Science questions are easier than they seem; almost everything I need to know to answer them is right in front of me.

Classifying passage format

You'll encounter three basic types of science passages that cover a variety of science topics:

» **Data representation:** Of the six passages in a typical science test, two or three are this type. They usually begin with a short paragraph that introduces the passage topic and defines terms followed by one or more tables, graphs, or diagrams that are chock-full of result data. Focus primarily on reading and evaluating the data in the tables and graphs (see the section,

"Analyzing Tables, Graphs, and Diagrams," later in this block) and only read the text if you need clarification of terms.

>> **Research summaries:** Two or three are research summaries. These passages include two or three separate experiments or studies to test one scientific topic. Each experiment or study has its own introductory text that conveys its specific setup. Make sure you focus on these paragraphs because these passages often contain questions that examine the relationship between two studies and compare and contrast their experimental design.

>> **Conflicting viewpoints:** One is this type. The conflicting-viewpoints passage usually begins with an introduction followed by text with headings like "Student 1," "Student 2," and "Student 3" or "Scientist 1" and "Scientist 2." These headings designate different ways of interpreting the information presented in the introduction. Most frequently, the opinions come from inexperienced students and therefore may contain information that contradicts known scientific truths.

Although these passage formats present information in slightly different ways, the general approach is the same regardless of the passage type:

>> Read the answer choices before you read the questions to determine the question type and where to focus.

>> Match information in the questions and answers to corresponding information in the passage.

Analyzing tables, graphics, and diagrams

Most passages test your ability to read and extract information from tables, graphs, or diagrams. In fact, data analysis is a primary assessment of the Science Test. We start with general guidelines for analyzing data:

>> **Examine the table, diagram, or graph as a whole.** Identify what the graphic is displaying (for example, drug dosages, reaction times, kinetic energy, or astronomical distances). You may need to skim the text immediately preceding the table or figure to get a full understanding of what's going on.

>> **Pay attention how the table or figure is labeled.**

>> **Note the units of measurement.** Tables and figures always present units of measurement very clearly. The axes on graphs are usually labeled, legends typically accompany diagrams, and column and row headings usually include the units.

>> **Look for trends in the data, noting any significant shifts.** The ACT Science Test frequently tests how data is related. Generally, a table or graph provides you with a clear picture of whether data is related directly or inversely or not at all.

● **Direct or positive correlation:** When two pieces of data increase at the same time or decrease at the same time, they are related directly.

● **Inverse or negative correlation:** When one piece of data increases at the same time another decreases or decreases at the same time another increases, those data points have an inverse relationship.

● **No correlation:** Data have no relationship or correlation when they act independently of one another.

>> **Observe corresponding data across multiple tables and figures in the passage.** Sometimes science questions require you to use data from one graph or table to draw conclusions about a data piece on another table or graph. Look for matching wording in the labels (column headings in tables and axis labels in graphs) to find where data from different tables and graphs may intersect with overlap.

Organizing Your Writing Test Essay

Writing a great essay is totally different from writing a really great ACT essay. A great essay is an artform: one you plan and think about for days, write for days, and edit for even more days. On the ACT, you have 40 minutes, so no one is expecting you to write something worthy of a literary award. This section helps you figure out what the test makers are looking for so you can give them exactly that.

Examining the prompt and creating a thesis

Responding to the ACT Writing Test prompt is somewhat like taking part in a debate. You'll read about an issue and then view three different perspectives. Your job is to get in on the action and form an opinion of your own.

The prompt may overwhelm you or bore you. It may include information that seems irrelevant. But no matter what, it poses a question worthy of careful consideration. Your first step is to review the information provided in the introduction and consider the three alternative positions that follow. Your second step is to form an opinion of your own. You don't really have to believe it yourself; you just need to write about it with confidence. The ACT people don't know you, and they certainly won't go to your house to ask you to explain yourself further. The key to starting a strong essay is taking a strong position right away. Here's what you need to do first:

1. **Read the question.**

2. **Pay attention to the first paragraph.**

   Typically, the first sentence of the prompt describes the issue. The following two sentences provide the position of its proponents and the view of the opposition. The third sentence gives the case of the opposition: Uniforms restrict freedom of expression. And the last sentence provides the consideration. Read this sentence carefully because it reveals the crux of the issue — in this prompt, the impact of requiring uniforms.

3. **Develop your own perspective regarding the question being posed by the prompt.**

   For example, if the issue is whether schools should require uniforms, do you think schools need to have uniforms? Or do you think students should come to school naked (just needed to wake you up here — did it work?). Don't just start writing before you decide your position, and never straddle both sides of an issue without coming out with a clear opinion.

4. **Compare your perspective with those already provided.**

   Maybe your perspective is very similar to one of the three provided, or maybe it's entirely different. Your essay only has to contain elements of one perspective; you aren't required to analyze all three.

By now you've read the prompt and all three perspectives, and you probably identify with one or two of them more than the others. Even if you don't, the time has come to put your own feelings about the issue down on paper. Remember that the ACT folks don't care what you really feel; they just want an essay, and they want one pronto!

REMEMBER

In your first sentence, never tell the ACT folks the reasons why you agree or disagree with the prompt and perspectives. Instead, provide a hook that grabs readers' attention, state the key perspectives you'll examine, and then establish your position. For example, if you have personal experience with school uniforms, you might introduce your essay like this:

"When my school decided to drop its school uniform requirement, the decision was controversial throughout our community. The debate reflected conflicting perspectives about school uniforms around the country: Some people believe uniforms will improve the learning environment, and others argue that uniforms may restrict individual freedom of expression. I believe high schools should require uniforms because certain types of clothing can distract students, lead to school violence, and interfere with a student's ability to fit in."

Demonstrating key writing skills

If you want to write an ACT essay that pleases your readers, make sure you do all of the following:

TIP

>> **State and develop a perspective.** Establishing a perspective requires you to explain your thoughts using examples, reasons, and details.

>> **Organize ideas.** Organizing your thoughts and ideas requires you to present your ideas in a logical way, using transitional words and phrases and sequencing your ideas so that they build on each other.

The ACT Writing Test is a great time to use the five-paragraph essay format to organize your writing. If you read our example introduction in the preceding section, notice how the thesis statement sets up the three middle paragraphs: You write one paragraph about whether or not certain types of clothing can distract students, a second about whether clothing leads to school violence, and a third about whether clothing interfere with a student's ability to fit in. Then you have the conclusion to explain why uniforms are a good idea (if that's the position you take in your essay).

>> **Evaluate and analyze the perspectives given.** Use them to help you form your thesis and add depth to your discussion, but don't think you need to analyze each perspective in your essay.

>> **Consider the relationship between your perspective and at least one other.** This analysis demonstrates that you thoroughly understand a complex issue.

>> **Maintain focus.** Staying focused requires you to stay on topic and make sure you don't add thoughts that aren't related to the prompt question.

>> **Back your ideas with detailed supporting information.** Rely on anecdotes and examples from your own experience.

>> **Communicate clearly.** Communicating clearly requires you to use a variety of sentence structures and vocabulary, spell correctly, and use mainstream grammar and punctuation.

Block 3
Working Through Some Practice Questions

You didn't think that we reviewed all that English, math, reading, science, and writing in Block 2 so you could lord your ACT knowledge over your friends, did you? Here we show you just how knowing the material in Block 2 comes in handy for the ACT. This practice block has representative questions for each test on the ACT. After you complete each question, you can review your answer by reading the explanation that follows and flip to Block 2 for more background information if you need it.

English Practice Questions

Directions: Following are four paragraphs containing underlined portions. Alternate ways of stating the underlined portions follow the paragraphs. Choose the best alternative. If the original is the best way of stating the underlined portion, choose NO CHANGE. You also see questions that refer to the passage or ask you to reorder the sentences within the passage. These questions are identified by a number in a box. Choose the best answer.

Marian Anderson: Groundbreaking Singer and Friend of First Ladies

[1] Marian Anderson possibly will have the greatest influence opening doors and gaining
                                              1   2
well-deserved opportunities for other African American singers than anyone else to date so far.
                                                                                            3
[2] Anderson, born in Philadelphia, Pennsylvania, had an early interest in music. [3] She learns
                                                                                            4
to play the piano and was singing in the church at the age of six. [4] She gave her first concert
at age eight, when she was still a young child.
                 5

[5] In 1925, Anderson won a concert hosted by the New York Philharmonic, beating out <u>no less than</u> 300 singers. [6] <u>It launched her career but,</u> America was not quite ready for her
6   7
fantastic voice, personality, or racial heritage.

In 1936, the White House <u>asking her</u> to give a performance. She confessed that this occasion
8
was <u>different than</u> other concerts because she was very nervous. She and Eleanor Roosevelt
9
became <u>close friends, but</u> this friendship <u>between she and the First Lady became</u> evident when
10   11
Anderson was snubbed by the Daughters of the American Revolution (DAR). The DAR refused to
let Anderson perform in Constitution Hall <u>in 1939, the White House</u> made arrangements for Ms.
12
Anderson to sing on the steps of the Lincoln Memorial instead.[13]

In 1977, First Lady Rosalynn Carter presented Marian Anderson with a Congressional Gold <u>Medal, making Ms. Anderson the first African American</u> to receive such an honor. Later she was
14
inducted into the Women's Hall of Fame in Seneca Falls, New York.[15]

1. **(A)** NO CHANGE

   (B) has had

   (C) has

   (D) is having

Because Marian Anderson's influence has already been felt, future tense isn't appropriate. Ms. Anderson has influenced and continues to influence. The verb tense that shows past action that continues or may continue into the present and beyond is present perfect, so the correct answer is (B).

2. **(F)** NO CHANGE

   (G) a greater

   (H) one of the greatest

   (J) a great

You need to read the entire sentence before deciding on an answer. If you read "the greatest influence" all by itself, it sounds correct. However, if you continue to read the sentence, you find the comparative *than*. You cannot say "the greatest influence than" but rather "a greater influence than." The correct answer is (G).

REMEMBER

Be very careful to read the entire sentence. You may save a few seconds by reading only the underlined portion, but you'll sacrifice a lot of points.

3. **(A)** NO CHANGE

   (B) dating so far

   (C) so far dated

   (D) OMIT the underlined portion.

To date and *so far* are redundant; they mean the same thing. You can use one or the other but not both. (Quick! Notify the Department of Redundancy Department!) The correct answer is (D).

4. (F) NO CHANGE

   (G) has been learning

   (H) learned

   (J) is learning

Because Marian Anderson is no longer six years old, the sentence requires the past tense, *learned. Hint:* If you aren't sure of the tense, check out the rest of the sentence. You're told that Ms. Anderson "was singing," meaning the situation occurred in the past. So the correct answer is (H).

5. (A) NO CHANGE

   (B) still a young child

   (C) still young

   (D) DELETE the underlined portion and end the sentence with a period.

A person who is eight is still a young child — duh! The underlined portion is superfluous, unnecessary. Eliminate it. The period is necessary to finish the sentence. The correct answer is (D).

6. (F) NO CHANGE

   (G) less than

   (H) fewer than

   (J) no fewer than

Use *fewer* to describe plural nouns, as in fewer brain cells, for example. Use *less* to describe singular nouns, like less intelligence. Because *singers* is a plural noun, use *fewer* rather than *less*. The correct answer is (J).

REMEMBER

If you picked Choice (H), you fell for the trap. You forgot to reread the sentence with your answer inserted. The meaning of the whole sentence changes with the phrase "fewer than 300 singers." In that case, you're diminishing the winner's accomplishment. The tone of the passage is one of respect. The author is impressed that Ms. Anderson beat out "no fewer than 300 singers." Keep in mind that you must make your answers fit the overall tone or attitude of the passage. If a passage is complimentary, be sure that your answers are, too.

7. (A) NO CHANGE

   (B) Launching her career,

   (C) The win launched her career, but

   (D) Upon launching it,

TIP

Be very suspicious of that two-letter rascal *it*. Always double-check *it* out because *it* is so often misused and abused. It must refer to one specific noun: "Where is the book? Here it is." In Question 7, *it* doesn't have a clear reference. It could mean that winning the concert launched her career, or it may seem that the New York Philharmonic launched her career. Another problem with Choice (A) is that pesky comma. It belongs before *but*, not after *it*. Choices (B) and (D) sound as if America launched Ms. Anderson's career: "Upon launching it . . . America was not quite ready . . . ." A beginning phrase always describes the sentence's subject. Be sure to go back and reread the entire sentence with your answer inserted. Because Choice (C) clarifies exactly what launched Anderson's career, it is the correct answer.

8. **(F)** NO CHANGE

   (G) asked her

   (H) was asking her

   (J) asking

The original is a fragment, an incomplete sentence. It tries to fool you into thinking that *asking* is the verb, but *ing* words all by themselves with no helping verbs to assist them can't work as verbs. The remedy is to change *asking* to the simple past verb *asked*. Because the sentence gives you a specific date, you know that the event happened at one point in the past. Therefore, Choice (H) is wrong. The White House wasn't in a continuous state of asking Ms. Anderson. So the correct answer is (G).

9. **(A)** NO CHANGE

   (B) different from

   (C) differed from

   (D) more different than

Standard English says *different from* rather than *different than*. Choice (D) adds more to the sentence to try to make *than* sound like a proper comparison term, but its addition also changes the meaning of the sentence. The White House concert wasn't more different than other concerts. It was simply different from other concerts that weren't as anxiety-provoking. The correct answer is (B).

REMEMBER

Choice (C) changes *than* to *from*, but it introduces another verb into a sentence that already has a verb. You may not notice the problem if you don't reread the sentence with Choice (C) inserted. Always reread the sentence with your answer choice inserted before you mark the answer on your sheet to make sure you haven't missed something important.

10. **(F)** NO CHANGE

    (G) close friends, and

    (H) close friends — which

    (J) close and friendly,

The clause "but this friendship . . . became evident . . ." makes no sense in the context. Use *but* only to indicate opposition or change; use a comma and the word *and* to add to and continue a thought. The correct answer is (G).

11. **(A)** NO CHANGE

    (B) between the First Lady and she became

    (C) between her and the First Lady became

    (D) OMIT the underlined portion.

The pronoun is the problem in this question. *Between* is a preposition, which means that the pronoun and noun that come after it are objects of the preposition. Therefore, the pronoun has to be in objective form. The objective form of *she* is *her*. You can't omit the underlined words because the resulting clause has no verb. The correct answer is (C).

REMEMBER

Many students tend to choose "OMIT the underlined portion" every time they see it, because they believe it would not be a choice unless it were correct. Not so. If you decide to omit the underlined portion, be especially careful to reread the entire sentence. Often, omitting the underlined portion makes nonsense out of the sentence.

12. (F) NO CHANGE

(G) in 1939; however, the White House

(H) in 1939 but the White House

(J) in 1939. Although the White House

To answer this question, you must correct the comma splice in the original sentence. You can't use a comma all by itself to join two independent clauses (complete sentences) in one sentence. You could separate them by putting a period after 1939 and capitalizing *the*. The answers don't give you that option, though. Choice (J) separates the clauses with a period, but adding *although* makes the second sentence a fragment. Another way to join two independent clauses together is with a semicolon. Choice (G) changes the comma to a semicolon and adds *however* for a smooth transition to the next thought. It properly places a comma after *however*, too. Choice (H) lacks a necessary comma before *but*. The correct answer is (G).

13. The author is considering inserting a sentence that presents a short list of other venues where Marian Anderson performed during her career. Would that insertion be appropriate here?

(A) Yes, because the primary purpose of this paragraph is to emphasize the great number of places where Marian Anderson performed.

(B) Yes, because it's always better to include many specific examples to advance an idea.

(C) No, because the paragraph is about the obstacles that Marian Anderson had to overcome rather than the number of concert halls she performed in.

(D) No, because providing a list of examples is never appropriate in an essay about a person's life.

When you see one of these "yes, yes, no, no" questions on the English Test, figure out the short answer to the question. Would a list of venues be appropriate? Probably not. (Please. The rest is boring enough without having to read through a list of concert venues.) Ignore the yes answers for now and focus on the no choices. The paragraph seems to focus on the racial prejudice Anderson experienced rather than the number of places she performed in. So the correct answer is (C).

REMEMBER

You can be pretty certain that Choices (B) and (D) are wrong. Both of them contain debatable words, such as *always* and *never*, that should raise a red flag for you. If you're thinking of choosing an answer that contains one of these all-encompassing words that leaves no room for exception, first make sure that the position is justified.

14. (F) NO CHANGE

(G) Medal, being the first African American

(H) Medal; the first African American

(J) Medal, the first African American

The original is okay the way it's written. The other choices make it sound like the medal was the first African American to receive such an honor. Choice (H) adds insult to injury by using a semi-icolon to do a comma's job. Note that the job of the semicolon is to separate two independent sentences; each sentence could stand alone. The correct answer is (F).

REMEMBER

Don't forget that the sentence doesn't have to have an error. About 20 percent of the time the underlined portion requires NO CHANGE.

15. If the author of this passage were to add the following lines to the article, where would they be most logically placed?

It was an era of racial prejudice, a time when people were still legally excluded from jobs, housing, and even entertainment merely because of their race. Thus, the early promise of success seemed impossible until something amazing for the times happened.

(A) After Sentence 2

(B) After Sentence 6

(C) After Sentence 3

(D) After Sentence 5

You know from the answer options to look only in the first two paragraphs. Because the first sentence of the addition talks about racial prejudice, look in the beginning of the passage for something that mentions Marian Anderson's race. That topic is specifically discussed only in Sentence 6. So the correct answer is (B).

REMEMBER

Be sure to go back to the passage and reread the entire paragraph with the new lines inserted to make sure that they make sense.

TIP

If you find yourself wasting too much time on a question like this one, your best bet is to eliminate answers if you can, guess, and move on. *Remember:* The ACT doesn't penalize you for wrong answers. Marking a guess for any question that has you stumped is to your advantage.

Math Practice Questions

Directions: Each of the following questions has five answer choices. Choose the best answer for each question.

1. $\dfrac{\left(a^4 \times a^3\right)^2}{a^4} =$

   (A) a^{36}

   (B) a^{10}

   (C) a^9

   (D) a^6

   (E) a^4

First, do the operation inside the parentheses. When you multiply like bases, you add the exponents: $a^4 \times a^3 = a^7$. When you have a power outside the parentheses, you multiply the exponents: $\left(a^7\right)^2 = a^{14}$. Finally, when you divide by like bases, you subtract the exponents: $a^{14} \div a^4 = a^{14-4} = a^{10}$. The correct answer is Choice (B).

WARNING

If you picked Choice (D), you fell for a trap answer. If you said $a^4 \times a^3 = a^{12}$ and $a^{(12)(2)} = a^{24}$, you may have divided a^{24} by a^4 and gotten a^6. If you chose Choice (A), you fell for another trap. You may have reasoned that $a^4 \times a^3 = a^{12}$. Because 12 squared is 144, you may have thought that $a^{(13)^2} = a^{144}$ and that $a^{144} \div a^4 = a^{30}$.

All these trap answers are intentional, put there to test whether you know how to perform operations with exponents. If you're still confused about how to multiply and divide like bases, turn to Block 2.

2. The ratio of knives to forks to spoons in a silverware drawer is 3:4:5. Which of the following could be the total number of knives, forks, and spoons in the drawer?

   (F) 60

   (G) 62

   (H) 64

   (J) 65

   (K) 66

The total number of utensils must be a multiple of the sum of the numbers of the ratios. In other words, add $3 + 4 + 5 = 12$. The total must be a multiple of 12. Only one answer choice, 60, divides evenly by 12, so you know the correct answer is Choice (F).

3. An usher passes out 60 percent of his programs before the intermission and 40 percent of the remainder after the intermission. At the end of the evening, what percent of the original number of programs does the usher have left?

   (A) 60

   (B) 40

   (C) 24

   (D) 16

   (E) 0

Whenever you have a percentage problem, plug in 100 for the original total. Assume that the usher begins with 100 programs. If he passes out 60 percent of them, he has passed out 60, leaving him with 40. Now comes the tricky part. After the intermission, the usher passes out 40 percent of the remaining programs: 40 percent of 40 is 16 ($0.4 \times 40 = 16$) and $40 - 16 = 24$. So the correct answer is Choice (C).

WARNING

Did you fall for the trap answer in Choice (E)? If you thought the usher first passed out 60 programs and then passed out the remaining 40, you believed that he had no programs left at the end of the evening. The word *remainder* is the key to this problem. The usher didn't pass out 40 percent of his original total, but 40 percent of the remaining programs.

If you chose Choice (D), you made a careless mistake. The number 16 represents the percentage of programs the usher passed out after the intermission. The question asks for the percent of programs the usher had left. We suggest that you circle the portion of the question that tells you what you're looking for. When you double-check your work, review this circled portion first.

4. A salesman makes a commission of $1.50 per shirt sold and $2.50 per pair of pants sold. In one pay period, he sold 10 more shirts than pairs of pants. If his total commission for the pay period was $215, what was the total number of shirts and pairs of pants he sold?

(F) 40

(G) 50

(H) 60

(J) 110

(K) 150

Let x be the number of pairs of pants the salesman sold. The number of shirts is $x + 10$ (because the problem tells you that the salesman sold 10 more shirts than pairs of pants). Set up the following equation:

$$\$1.50(x + 10) + \$2.50(x) = \$215$$

Now just follow these steps to solve for x:

1. **Multiply:** $1.50x + 15 + 2.50x = 215$

2. **Combine like terms:** $4.00x + 15 = 215$

3. **Isolate the x on one side:** $4.00x = 215 - 15$

4. **Subtract:** $4.00x = 200$

5. **Divide:** $x = 200 \div 4$, or $x = 50$

WARNING

If you answered with Choice (G), you fell for the trap answer (after all that hard work)! Remember to go back and reread what the question is asking for. In this case, it wants to know the total number of pants and shirts sold. So you're not done working yet. If x (which equals 50) is the number of pairs of pants, then $x + 10$ (which is 60) is the number of shirts sold. (Note that 60 is a trap answer as well.) Combine $50 + 60$ to get the right answer, 110. The correct answer is Choice (J).

5. Kim and Scott work together stuffing envelopes. Kim works twice as fast as Scott. Together they stuff 2,100 envelopes in four hours. How long would Kim, working alone, take to stuff 175 envelopes?

    (A) 20 minutes

    (B) 30 minutes

    (C) 1 hour

    (D) 3 hours

    (E) 6 hours

The ratio of Kim's work to Scott's work is 2:1. In other words, she does two out of every three envelopes. Scott does one out of every three envelopes, for a total of 700 envelopes $(2,100 \div 3)$. Scott stuffs 700 envelopes in four hours, and Kim stuffs 1,400 $(2,100 - 700 = 1,400)$ in four hours. Divide 1,400 by 4 to find that Kim produces 350 stuffed envelopes per hour. 175 is one-half of 350. Therefore, in one half-hour (or 30 minutes), Kim can stuff 175 envelopes. The correct answer is Choice (B).

TIP

When you encounter a word problem like this one, don't start thinking about equations immediately. Talking through the problem may help you more than creating a bunch of equations.

6. If $DC = 6$ and point O is the center of the circle, what is the shaded area in the figure?

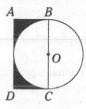

    (F) $72 - 18\pi$

    (G) $72 - 36\pi$

    (H) 9π

    (J) $36 - 18\pi$

    (K) $36 - 36\pi$

A *shaded area* is the leftover portion of a figure. To find a shaded area, you usually find the total area and the unshaded area and then subtract. In this figure, the shaded area is the total area of rectangle *ABCD* less the area of half the circle. If the side *DC* is 6, the radius of the circle is also 6.

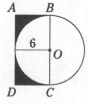

REMEMBER

The area of a circle is πr^2; therefore, the area of this circle is $\pi 6^2$ or 36π. Be careful to remember that you're working only with a semicircle. The shaded area subtracts only half the area of the circle, so you know you have to subtract 18π. That immediately narrows the answers to Choices (F) and (J).

Next, find the area of the rectangle. (The area of a rectangle equals length × width.) The width of DC is 6. Because the radius of the circle is 6, the diameter of the circle is 12. So BC, the diameter of the circle, is the same as the length of the rectangle. To find the area of the rectangle, simply multiply: $6 \times 12 = 72$. Finally, subtract: $72 - 18\pi$. The correct answer is Choice (F).

7. When $5a^2 + (5a)^2 = 120$, what is the value of a?

(A) 2

(B) 3

(C) 4

(D) 5

(E) 6

First, deal with the parentheses: $(5a)^2 = 5a \times 5a$, which is $25a^2$. Then add like terms: $25a^2 + 5a^2 = 30a^2$. Finally, solve the equation for a:

$$5a^2 + (5a)^2 = 120$$
$$30a^2 = 120$$
$$a^2 = 120 \div 30$$
$$a^2 = 4$$
$$a = 2$$

The correct answer is Choice (A).

WARNING

Choice (C) is the trap answer. If you divided 120 by 30 and got 4, you may have picked Choice (C), forgetting that 4 represented a^2, not a.

Of course, you also could simply plug in each answer choice and work backward to solve this problem. Start with the middle value in the answer choices. If $a = 4$, then

$$5(4)^2 + (5 \times 4)^2 =$$
$$5(16) + 20^2 =$$
$$+ 400 = 480$$
$$480 \neq 120$$

The value of Choice (C) is too great, so try Choices (A) and (B), which are smaller numbers.

8. Three times as much as $\frac{1}{3}$ less than $3x$ is how much in terms of x?

(F) $9x$

(G) $8x$

(H) $6x$

(J) x

(K) $\frac{1}{3}x$

Working backward in this type of problem is usually the easiest way to solve it. One-third less than $3x$ is $2x$. You can calculate it this way: $3x - \frac{1}{3}(3x) = 3x - x = 2x$. Then just multiply by 3: $3 \times 2x = 6x$. The correct answer is Choice (H).

9. The following chart shows the weights of junior high school students. What is the sum of the mode and the median weights?

Weight in Pounds	Number of Students
110	4
120	2
130	3
140	2

(A) 230 pounds

(B) 235 pounds

(C) 250 pounds

(D) 255 pounds

(E) 258 pounds

This question tests vocabulary as much as it tests math. The *mode* is the most frequently repeated number. In this case, 110 is repeated more often than any other term. The *median* is the middle term when the numbers are arranged in order. Here you have 110, 110, 110, 110, 120, 120, 130, 130, 130, 140, 140. Of these 11 numbers, the sixth one, 120, is the median. And $110 + 120 = 230$, so the correct answer is Choice (A).

TIP

Don't confuse *median* with *mean*. The *mean* is the average. You get the mean by adding all the terms and then dividing by the number of terms. If you confused median with mean, you'd really be in a quandary, because the sum of the mean and the mode is 232.73 and that answer isn't an option. If you picked Choice (B), you fell into a different trap. You found that 125 was the median by adding the first and last terms and dividing by 2. Sorry. To find the median, you have to write out all the terms from least to greatest (all four 110s, both 120s, and so on) and then locate the middle term.

10. Points *E*, *D*, and *A* are colinear. The ratio of the area of △*EBD* to △*ABD* is

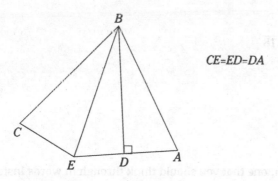

CE=ED=DA

(F) 3:2

(G) 3:1

(H) 2:1

(J) 1:1

(K) 1:2

The area of a triangle is $\frac{1}{2}bh$. The base of *EBD* is *ED*. *ED* is equal to *AD*, which is the base of △*ABD*. The bases of the two triangles are equal. The heights are equal, as well. By definition, the height of a triangle is a line from the tallest point perpendicular to the base. If the triangles have the same base and the same height, the ratio of their areas is 1:1. So the correct answer is Choice (J).

11. Given this equation $\begin{array}{r} 95c5 \\ +3cbd \\ \hline ab3a2 \end{array}$, solve for the sum of $a + b + c$.

(A) 15

(B) 14

(C) 13

(D) 12

(E) 11

TIP

If you're rushed for time, this problem is a good one to skip and come back to later. Mark a guess on your answer sheet, put a big checkmark next to the questions in your test booklet, and evaluate the question after you've finished the last math question. Remember that the ACT doesn't assess a penalty for wrong answers. Never leave an answer blank. Even a wild guess is worthwhile. However, if you do a few of these practice problems, you'll be surprised at how quickly you can get them right.

Don't panic. This problem is much easier than it appears. Start with the right-hand column, the ones or units column: $5 + c = $ a number that ends in 2. You know that the 2 must be a 12 instead of just a 2 because you can't add a positive number to 5 and get 2, which means $c = 7$. Jot down $c = 7$.

When you carry the 1 to the tens column, you get $1 + 7$, which is 8, and $8 + b = a$. You don't know a yet ... or do you? Go to the far-left column (the thousands column). If the answer is $ab3\ a2$, the variable a must equal 1. You can't add two four-digit numbers and get 20,000-something. The most you can get is 10,000-something (for example, $9,999 + 9,999 = 19,998$). Now you know that a is 1. Jot down $a = 1$.

Go back to the tens column: $1 + 7 = 8$ and $8 + b = 11$ (it can't be 1; it must be 11). Therefore, $b = 3$. Carry the 1 to the hundreds column: $1 + 5 = 6$ and $6 + c$ (which is 7) = 13. Yes, this is true — a good check. Carry the 1 to the next column: $1 + 9 = 10$ and $10 + 3$ is 13, which is what we said ab was in the first place. Therefore, $c = 7$, $b = 3$, $a = 1$, and $7 + 3 + 1 = 11$. The correct answer is Choice (E).

The most common mistake that students make on this type of problem is forgetting to carry the 1 to the next column. Double-check that you have done so.

REMEMBER

12. $a\beta b = \dfrac{1}{a} + \dfrac{1}{b}$ What is the value of $\dfrac{2}{15}\beta\dfrac{2}{18}$?

(F) 14

(G) 14.5

(H) 15

(J) 16

(K) 16.5

This problem is a symbolism problem, one that you should think through in words instead of heading for an equation. The symbol β indicates that you add the reciprocals of the two numbers. For example, the reciprocal of a is $\dfrac{1}{a}$, and the reciprocal of b is $\dfrac{1}{b}$. Therefore, add the reciprocals of $\dfrac{2}{15}$ and $\dfrac{2}{18}$. $\dfrac{15}{2} + \dfrac{18}{2} = \dfrac{33}{2} = 16.5$. The correct answer is Choice (K).

The β has this meaning for this problem only. The meanings of symbols vary from problem to problem; always read the problems carefully.

REMEMBER

Reading Practice Questions

Directions: Answer each question based on what is stated or implied in the passage.

Passage 1 — Literary Narrative

This passage is adapted from the Robert Louis Stevenson novel *Kidnapped*.

Meanwhile such of the wounded as could move came clambering out of the fore-scuttle and began to help; while the rest that lay helpless in their bunks harrowed me with screaming and begging to be saved.

The captain took no part. It seemed he was struck stupid. He stood holding by the shrouds, talking to himself and groaning out aloud whenever the ship hammered on the rock. His brig was like wife and child to him; he had looked on, day by day, at the mishandling of poor Ransome; but when it came to the brig, he seemed to suffer along with her.

All the time of our working at the boat, I remember only one other thing; that I asked Alan, looking across at the shore, what country it was; and he answered, it was the worst possible for him, for it was a land of the Campbells.

We had one of the wounded men told off to keep a watch upon the seas and cry us warning. Well, we had the boat about ready to be launched, when this man sang out pretty shrill: "For God's sake, hold on!" We knew by his tone that it was something more than ordinary; and sure enough; there followed a sea so huge that it lifted the brig right up and canted her over on her beam. Whether the cry came too late or my hold was too weak, I know not; but at the sudden tilting of the ship I was cast clean over the bulwarks into the sea.

I went down, and drank my fill; and then came up, and got a blink of the moon; and then down again. They say a man sinks the third time for good. I cannot be made like other folk, then; for I would not like to write how often I went down or how often I came up again. All the while, I was being hurled along, and beaten upon and choked, and then swallowed whole, and the thing was so distracting to my wits, that I was neither sorry nor afraid.

Presently, I found I was holding to a spar, which helped me somewhat. And then all of a sudden I was in quiet water, and began to come to myself.

It was the spare yard I had got hold of, and I was amazed to see how far I had traveled from the brig. I hailed her indeed; but it was plain she was already out of cry. She was still holding together; but whether or not they had yet launched the boat, I was too far off and too low down to see.

While I was hailing the brig, I spied a tract of water lying between us, where no great waves came, but which yet boiled white all over, and bristled in the moon with rings and bubbles. Sometimes the whole tract swung to one side, like the tail of a live serpent; sometimes, for a glimpse, it all would disappear and then boil up again. What it was I had no guess, which for the time increased my fear of it; but I now know it must have been the roost or tide race, which carried me away so fast and tumbled me about so cruelly, and at last, as if tired of that play, had flung me and spare yard upon its landward margin.

1. The narrator compares the ship to the captain's wife and child to:

(A) lament the captain's long separation from his family.

(B) demonstrate the difficulty the captain has keeping focused on his job.

(C) predict the captain's future madness.

(D) show the depth of the connection the captain has to his ship.

The focus of the second paragraph is on how the captain is upset by the condition of his ship. To compare his ship to his wife and child is to show how much he loves the ship and, thus, to emphasize the deep attachment he has to the vessel. So the correct answer is Choice (D).

2. By saying that he "got a blink of the moon" in the fifth paragraph, the narrator most nearly means that:

(F) he foresaw his own demise.

(G) he saw the sky as he came up out of the water to get air.

(H) he was hallucinating as he was drowning.

(J) a barely perceptible quarter moon hung low in the sky.

The first line of the fifth paragraph describes the narrator's dunking and near drowning. He was bobbing up and down in the water, going under the sea and then coming up for air, at which point he saw the moon. Make sure you answer the question in the context in which you find the statement; don't use your own common sense. And if you picked Choice (J), you chose an answer that provided too much unjustifiable detail to be right. The correct answer is Choice (G).

Passage 2 — Social Science

Multinational corporations frequently have difficulty explaining to politicians, human rights groups, and (perhaps most important) their consumer base why they do business with, and even seek closer business ties to, countries whose human rights records are considered very bad by United States standards. The CEOs say that in the business trenches, the issue of human rights must effectively be detached from the wider spectrum of free trade.

Discussion of the uneasy alliance between trade and human rights has trickled down from the boardrooms of large multinational corporations to the consumer on the street who, given the wide variety of products available to him, is eager to show support for human rights by boycotting the products of a company he feels does not do enough to help its overseas workers.

International human rights organizations also are pressuring the multinationals to push for more humane working conditions in other countries and to, in effect, develop a code of business conduct that must be adhered to if the American company is to continue working with the overseas partner.

The President, in drawing up a plan for what he calls the "economic architecture of our times," wants economists, business leaders, and human rights groups to work together to develop a set of principles that the foreign partners of United States corporations will voluntarily embrace. Human rights activists, angry at the unclear and indefinite plans for implementing such rules, charge that their agenda is being given low priority by the State Department. The President strongly denies their charges, arguing that each situation is approached on its merits without prejudice, and hopes that all the groups can work together to develop principles based on empirical research rather than political fiat, emphasizing that the businesses with experience in the field must initiate the process of developing such guidelines. Business leaders, while paying lip service to the concept of these principles, secretly fight against their formal endorsement as they fear such "voluntary" concepts may someday be given the force of law. Few business leaders have forgotten the Sullivan Principles, in which a set of voluntary rules regarding business conduct with South Africa (giving benefits to workers and banning apartheid in the companies that worked with U.S. partners) became legislation.

3. Which of the following best states the central idea of the passage?

(A) Politicians are quixotic in their assessment of the priorities of the State Department.

(B) Multinational corporations have little, if any, influence on the domestic policies of their overseas partners.

(C) Disagreement exists between the desires of human rights activists to improve the working conditions of overseas workers and the practical approach taken by the corporations.

(D) It is inappropriate to expect foreign corporations to adhere to American standards.

The main idea of the passage is usually stated in the first sentence or two. The first sentence of this passage discusses the difficulties that corporations have in explaining their business ties to certain countries to politicians, human rights groups, and consumers. From this statement, you may infer that those groups disagree with the policies of the corporations. So the correct answer is Choice (C).

TIP

Did you pick Choice (A) just because of the hard word, *quixotic*? It's human nature (we're all so insecure) to think that the hard word we don't know must be the right answer, but it isn't always so. Never choose an answer just because it has a word you can't define unless you're sure that all the answers with words you can define are wrong. *Quixotic* means idealistic, impractical (think of the fictional character Don Quixote tilting at windmills). The President's belief is not the main idea of the passage.

REMEMBER

Just because a statement is (or may be) true doesn't necessarily mean that it's the correct answer to a question. Many of the answer choices to a big picture question in particular often are true or at least look plausible. To answer a main-idea question, pretend that a friend of yours just came up behind you and said, "Hey, what'cha reading there?" Your first response is the main idea: "Oh, I read this passage about how corporations are getting grief from politicians and other groups because they do business with certain countries." Before you look at the answer choices, predict in your own words what the main idea is. You'll be pleasantly surprised how close your prediction is to the correct answer (and you won't be confused by all the other plausible-looking answer choices).

TIP

Choice (D) is a moral value, a judgment call. Who's to say what's appropriate and what's inappropriate? An answer that passes judgment, one that says something is morally right or morally wrong, is almost never the correct answer on the ACT.

4. Which of the following statements about the Sullivan Principles can best be inferred from the passage?

(F) They had a detrimental effect on the profits of those corporations doing business with South Africa.

(G) They represented an improper alliance between political and business groups.

(H) They placed the needs of the foreign workers over those of the domestic workers whose jobs would therefore be in jeopardy.

(J) They will have a chilling effect on future adoption of voluntary guidelines.

Choice (F) is the major trap here. Perhaps you assumed that because the companies seem to dislike the Sullivan Principles, they hurt company profits. However, the passage doesn't say anything about profits. Maybe the companies still made good profits but objected to the Sullivan Principles on principle. The companies just may not have wanted such governmental intervention even if profits didn't decrease. If you picked Choice (F), you read too much into the question and probably didn't read the rest of the answer choices.

In Choice (J), the phrase "chilling effect" means a negative or discouraging effect. Think of something with a chilling effect as leaving you cold. Because few corporations have forgotten the Sullivan Principles, you may infer that these principles will discourage the companies from agreeing to voluntary principles in the future. Thus, the correct answer is (J).

TIP

To get this question correct, you really need to understand the whole passage. If you didn't know what was going on here, you'd be better off just to guess and move on. An inference question usually means you have to read between the lines; you can't just go back to one specific portion of the passage and get the answer quickly.

Passage 3 — Humanities

Many people believe that the existence of lawyers and lawsuits represents a relatively recent phenomenon. The opinion that many hold regarding lawyers, also known as attorneys, is that they are insincere and greedy. Lawyers are often referred to as "ambulance chasers" or by other pejorative expressions.

Despite this negativity, lawyers are also known for their fights for civil rights, due process of law, and equal protection. Lawyers were instrumental in desegregating the institutions in our society and in cleaning up the environment. Most legislators at the local, state, and federal level of government are lawyers because they generally have a firm understanding of justice and the proper application of statutory and case law.

Lawyers are traditionally articulate public speakers, or orators, too. One of the finest legal orators was Marcus Tullius Cicero, who was an intellectually distinguished, politically savvy, and incredibly successful Roman lawyer. Cicero lived from 143–106 B.C. and was one of only a few Roman intellectuals credited with the flowering of Latin literature that largely occurred during the last decades of the Roman republic.

Cicero's compositions have been compared to the works of Julius Caesar. Their writings have customarily been included in the curriculum wherever Latin is studied. Cicero was a lifelong student of government and philosophy and a practicing politician. He was a successful lawyer whose voluminous speeches, letters, and essays tend to have the same quality that people usually associate with pleading a case. His arguments are well structured, eloquent, and clear. Cicero perfected the complex, balanced, and majestic sentence structure called "periodic," which was imitated by later writers from Plutarch in the Renaissance to Churchill in the 20th century.

5. *Pejorative*, as it appears in the last line of the first paragraph, most nearly means:

(A) comic.

(B) dishonest.

(C) self-serving.

(D) uncomplimentary.

Get clues for answering this question from the information around the word. The passage classifies "ambulance chaser" as a pejorative expression. In the next sentence, the author uses the phrase "this negativity" to refer to the act of using pejorative statements for attorneys. Therefore, *pejorative* must have a negative connotation. You can eliminate Choice (A) — even though the thought of an overweight attorney running after a screaming ambulance may make you laugh. Plug the remaining choices into the sentence to see which one makes the best substitute for *pejorative.* The obvious answer is *uncomplimentary.* So the correct answer is Choice (D).

If you picked Choice (B) or (C), you were probably thinking of words that describe the way that the author says many people think of attorneys. *Dishonest* is a synonym for *insincere,* and *self-serving* has a meaning that's similar to *greedy.* Trap answers like Choices (B) and (C) are why you must read your answers in the context of the sentence. By doing so, you see that *pejorative* describes the expressions that others give to attorneys, not the attorneys themselves.

6. Which of these, according to the author, is a way that lawyers have positively contributed to society?

(F) They have fought legislation designed to clean up the environment.

(G) They have proposed laws to make "ambulance chasing" illegal.

(H) They have taught public speaking skills to disadvantaged youth.

(J) They have advocated for integration of public institutions.

The author covers the positive attributes of lawyers in the second paragraph, which mentions their contributions to cleaning up the environment and promoting integration. The passage doesn't say anything about the legalization of "ambulance chasing" or teaching public speaking, so you can eliminate Choices (G) and (H). Choice (F) is a little tricky if you don't read it carefully. Because Choice (F) says that attorneys have fought rather than promoted cleaning up the environment, it says just the opposite of what the passage states. So Choice (J) is the correct answer.

Passage 4 — Natural Science

Biomes are the major biological divisions of the earth. Biomes are characterized by an area's climate and the particular organisms that live there. The living organisms make up the "biotic" components of the biome, and everything else makes up the "abiotic" components. The density and diversity of a biome's biotic components is called its "carrying capacity." The most important abiotic aspects of a biome are the amount of rainfall it has and how much its temperatures vary. More rain and more stable temperatures mean more organisms can survive. Usually, the wetter a biome is, the less its temperature changes from day to night or from summer to winter. Biomes include deserts, rain forests, forests, savannas, tundras, freshwater environments, and oceans.

Deserts are areas that get less than 10 inches of rain per year. Most deserts are hot (like the Sahara), but some are actually cold (like parts of Antarctica). Therefore, the thing that distinguishes deserts is their extreme dryness. The organisms that live in a desert need to be able to survive drastic temperature swings along with dry conditions, so the desert's carrying capacity is extremely low. Desert animals include reptiles like lizards and snakes and some arachnids like spiders and scorpions.

Freshwater environments and oceans are also biomes. The freshwater biome includes elements like rivers, lakes, and ponds. These areas are affected by temperature swings, the amount of available oxygen, and the speed of water flowing through them. All of these are affected by the larger climate area the freshwater biome is in, which also affects the biotic components. Algae, fish, amphibians, and insects are found in freshwater biomes. Oceans cover about 70 percent of the earth's surface, so they comprise the biggest biome. Temperature swings aren't nearly as wide in the oceans as they are on land, and there's plenty of water to go around. Therefore, the carrying capacity of the oceans is huge. The density and diversity of organisms isn't quite as high as in the tropical rain forest, but the total number of organisms in the oceans is much bigger than all of the terrestrial biomes put together.

7. Which of the following best presents the organization of the passage?

    (A) It first provides several terms related to biomes and then provides further illumination of the concepts by describing how they manifest in some biomes.

    (B) It starts with general definitions of biotic and abiotic and then provides evidence that not all biomes demonstrate both categories.

    (C) It begins with descriptions of several weather events and then shows examples of these events in a variety of biomes.

    (D) It divides the earth into several biomes and then provides a thorough description of each of those biomes.

Apply process of elimination. Look for wrong elements in the answer choices. Choice (B) is untrue; the passage begins with definitions of biotic and abiotic, but it doesn't talk about biomes that don't contain both categories. The passage mentions weather types but doesn't describe them, so Choice (C) isn't right. The word "thorough" in Choice (D) is a red flag. The first paragraph lists several biomes, but the following paragraphs describe only a few of them, and the descriptions couldn't be classified as thorough. For example, they don't completely list the types of organisms that live in oceans.

The first paragraph provides general definitions of biomes, biotic, abiotic, and carrying capacity. The last two paragraphs provide more specific descriptions of the biotic and abiotic qualities of several biomes and how these qualities affect carrying capacity. Choice (A) is the best answer.

It's usually easier to spot wrong answer than right ones, so focus on finding what's wrong with answers. Then the correct choice will arise above the others.

REMEMBER

8. According to the passage, all of these elements affect the quality of a freshwater environment EXCEPT:

    (F) oxygen levels.

    (G) swings in temperature.

    (H) the larger climate in which it exists.

    (J) the policies of the country in which it exists.

The answer to this exception question comes straight from the passage. The third paragraph says that freshwater biomes are affected by temperature swings, the amount of available oxygen, and the speed of water flowing through them, so you can eliminate Choices (F), (G), and (H). The passage doesn't cover issues that are unrelated to the natural environment, so the correct answer is Choice (J).

The best way to answer exception questions is to turn the wording around a bit. For example, you can approach this question by asking yourself to choose the answer that states something that *doesn't* affect the quality of a freshwater environment.

TIP

Science Practice Questions

This section gives you a Science Test passage with twice the usual number of questions. On the actual ACT, the passages have only 6 or 7 questions, not 12 as in this section. We give you double the usual number to give you practice in the various ways the ACT can test the same basic points.

Directions: Based on the following science passage, answer the 12 questions.

Don't forget to read all the answer explanations after you're done!

Passage

By using electrical recording devices, scientists have shown that many cells in the part of the brain involved with processing visual information respond only to lines of a certain orientation. For example, some brain cells fire when vertical lines are present but do not respond to horizontal lines. Animals that rely on vision must have an entire set of cells so that at least some part of their brains responds when lines of a given orientation are present in their environment.

Scientists conducted several studies on *R. norvegicus domestica* (a species of rat commonly used in laboratory experimentation) to explore how much brain organization is affected by the animal's environment and investigate the role that environment plays in the development of rat vision. Over a period of 6 weeks, scientists exposed rat pups of various ages to a variety of visual environments: continuous exposure to vertical lines, continuous exposure to horizonal lines, continuous exposure to lines of both horizontal and vertical orientations, and continuous exposure to complete darkness. They then observed the subjects' behavior in mazes with horizontal and vertical obstacles and monitored and measured electrical activity from the visual part of the subjects' brains. The rat pups that were 6 weeks and 6 months old at the beginning of the study had been raised in *normal* environments (environments with uncontrolled exposure to various stimuli and light and dark patterns) from birth until that time. The results of the series of studies is provided in Table 1, which shows the study number, age of *R. norvegicus domestica* at the beginning of the study, the type of environmental factors imposed during the study, the corresponding percentage of brain activity when the subjects were exposed to horizonal and vertical stimuli after the study, and the subjects' ability to navigate obstacles in mazes.

TABLE 1

Study	Age of *R. norvegicus domestica*	Imposed Environmental Factor			% Brain Activity		Maze Navigation	
		Horizontal Line Exposure	Vertical Line Exposure	Complete Darkness	Horizontal Stimuli Exposure	Vertical Stimuli Exposure	Collide with Horizontal Obstacles	Collide with Vertical Obstacles
1	Newborn	yes	Yes	no	50	50	No	no
2	6 weeks	yes	Yes	no	50	50	No	no
3	Newborn	No	No	yes	5	5	Yes	yes
4	Newborn	no	yes	no	0	75	Yes	no
5	Newborn	yes	No	no	75	0	No	yes
6	6 months	No	No	yes	50	50	No	no
7	6 months	No	Yes	no	50	50	No	no
8	6 months	yes	No	no	50	50	No	no

Initial Analysis

This passage presents you with a short introduction and a single table that reports both procedure details and study results. You may be tempted to read through all that mess before you tackle the questions. Don't waste your time! All passages are best approached by skipping the passage and jumping right into answering the questions.

TIP

Use the information in the questions to direct you to the part of the passage you need to go to find the answers. If the question confuses you, get guidance from reading the answer choices. They can tell you what elements to focus on.

Questions

1. On the basis of Study 1, can newborn rat pups see vertical lines?

(A) No, because the newborn rat pups did not collide with vertical obstacles.

(B) No, because the newborn rat pups collided with horizontal obstacles.

(C) Yes, because the newborn rat pups collided with horizontal obstacles.

(D) Yes, because the newborn rat pups did not collide with vertical obstacles.

This "yes, yes, no, no" question type concerns Study 1. A quick glance at the answer choices tells you that the only data you need to consider is whether the pups collided with vertical and horizontal obstacles. Focus your attention on Table 1's last columns. The table clearly shows that the pups avoided collisions with both horizontal and vertical obstacles. Examine your answer choices more thoroughly. You can immediately eliminate Choices (B) and (C) because they're not true. The pups in Study 1 avoided the horizontal obstacles.

Now all you have to figure out is whether colliding with vertical obstacles indicates whether the pups can see vertical lines. Don't overthink this one. You don't have to worry that some groundbreaking study in Sweden may have revealed that the eye actually sees horizontal objects as vertical, and vice versa. The pups avoided the vertical objects, so they likely saw them. The best answer is Choice (D).

REMEMBER

Take the path of least resistance. Pick the most logical answer given the data in the passage and your own knowledge of the world.

2. Scientists place a 3-week-old rat pup that had been raised in an environment with both horizontal and vertical visual stimuli in a maze of vertical and horizontal obstacles. Which of the following is the most likely result?

(F) The rat pup collides with horizontal obstacles but avoids vertical obstacles.

(G) The rat pup collides with vertical obstacles but avoids horizontal obstacles.

(H) The rat pup collides with both vertical and horizontal obstacles.

(J) The rat pup avoids both vertical and horizontal obstacles.

If a newborn pup can get around the maze and a pup raised in an environment with exposure to both horizontal and vertical stimuli for six weeks can get around the maze, then you can logically conclude that a pup raised in a normal environment for three weeks would also be able to do so. Only Choice (J) has a pup that doesn't need a crash helmet, so it's your winner.

REMEMBER

Did you have Smart Students' Disease on this question and read more into the question? If you said, "Yeah, but what if . . ." and started imagining all sorts of horrible and unlikely possibilities ("Maybe the rat OD'd on cheese and staggered around . . ."), you made this problem much harder than it really was. Keep it simple, okay?

3. Scientists place a 6-month-old rat that had been raised in a normal environment in a maze of vertical and horizontal obstacles. Which of the following is the most likely result?

(A) The rat makes no attempt to get around the obstacles.

(B) The rat negotiates around both vertical and horizontal obstacles.

(C) The rat bumps into horizontal obstacles but gets around vertical obstacles.

(D) The rat bumps into vertical obstacles but gets around horizontal obstacles.

Did you try to answer this question based on Studies 1 and 2? Doing so worked for the previous question because it spoke of an age, 3 weeks, that was between newborn (Study 1) and 6 weeks (Study 2). Check the question for details. In this question, the rat is older than the oldest pup in Studies 1 and 2, meaning that you can't be sure that the present trend continues. (Common sense tells you that the trend probably will continue, but you must be able to distinguish between what will probably happen and what will necessarily happen.)

Skim the studies for ones that provide a more definitive answer. In Studies 6, 7, and 8, scientists took rats that had previously been exposed to a normal environment for six months and exposed them to a different environment for six weeks. Because the rat in this question didn't have to endure a different experience and the vision of the rats that were exposed to the different environments turned out okay, the rat that wasn't placed in such an environment should also be okay. So the correct answer is Choice (B).

TIP If you were really lost on this problem, you could eliminate Choice (A) right away because it's much too extreme. Answers with words like *rarely* and *infrequently* are right much more often than their dramatic counterparts like *no* and *never*. Because nothing indicates a favoring of vertical over horizontal lines, or vice versa, you can eliminate Choices (C) and (D) as well.

4. Which of the following was not under the direct control of the experimenters?

(F) the length of time that the rat spent in a controlled environment

(G) the percentage of measured brain activity in response to exposure to horizontal lines

(H) the age at which the rat was tested for visual response

(J) the types of obstacles placed in a maze

This is an experiment set-up question, which means you may need to read a little of the introductory material to answer it. When an experimental factor, or *variable,* is under the direct control of the experimenters, the experimenters can decide exactly how much (or what type) of that factor to use without having to depend on any intervening process. Choice (F) is clearly under the control of the experimenters. The experimenters can let the rat out of the maze (the environment) any time they want. Choice (J) is just as clear. The experimenters can throw in more vertical or horizontal obstacles at will.

Choice (H) is a little tougher to eliminate. You may think that the rat's age is up to the rat (or at least up to its parents), but the experimenters can decide exactly how old the rats have to be in order to be used in a certain part of the experiment.

By process of elimination, Choice (G) is correct. The experimenters can try to affect brain activity by changing the environment, but exactly how many brain cells respond depends on physiological factors outside the experimenters' control.

The basic science info covered in Question 4 comes into play in many different passages. *Independent variables* — Choices (F), (H), and (J), in this case — are those that experimenters can manipulate independently of any other factor. For example, the experimenter can change the time spent in the dark environment from six weeks to five weeks without changing the type of obstacles in the maze. A *dependent variable* — Choice (G) in this case — depends on what else was done in the experiment.

5. What is the relationship between Study 6 and Study 3?

   (A) An examination of the results of Study 6 and Study 3 shows that the effects of six weeks in darkness may depend on the rat's age at the time scientists place the subjects in complete darkness.

   (B) The rats in Study 3 were exposed to a different experimental environment than those in Study 6.

   (C) Study 6 extends the findings of Study 3 by showing that longer periods of darkness also change brain-cell activity.

   (D) Study 6 contradicts the findings of Study 3 by showing that, when rats are placed in darkness for a longer period of time, the maze navigation results found in Study 3 are altered.

You can dump Choices (B), (C), and (D) because they aren't true. The two studies imposed the same environmental condition, complete darkness, so Choice (B) is wrong. The other two answers are wrong because Study 6 used older rats (ones that have been alive for a longer period of time), but these rats, as well as those of Study 3, were in darkness for only six weeks.

Often, three answer options for science questions are obviously wrong. The only answer left is Choice (A), which is correct.

6. Some humans who have suffered brain injuries have been able to recover a lost brain function by having the brain reorganize itself. On the basis of all the rat-vision studies, which of the following humans would be most likely to recover a lost function through brain reorganization?

   (F) a 50-year-old man who suffers a stroke (lack of oxygen to a certain region of the brain)

   (G) an 80-year-old woman who suffers a stroke

   (H) a 30-year-old combat soldier who suffers a bullet wound in the brain

   (J) a baby who has had part of the left side of his brain surgically removed along with a tumor

Calm down, calm down — no one expects you to know exactly how each of these brain traumas affects brain functioning. Everything you need to answer this question is there in the passage. Plus, you can rely on what you know from your world experience to eliminate less logical answers to science questions. The key is to pick up on the ages. Which rats showed a change from the ordinary response pattern when the environment changed? The young rats. Similarly, a young human's brain is likely to be more flexible than that of an older human. Haven't you always pointed out to your parents not to be so narrow-minded and set in their ways? Choice (J), which features the youngest human, is the correct answer.

If you're almost having a stroke right now arguing with us, you probably didn't notice how carefully the question was worded: "Which of the following humans would be *most likely* to . . .?" True, you don't know for sure that the baby would have some lost brain function, but all you're asked is which of the answer choices is the most likely (and, no, "a student studying for the ACT" wasn't among them).

7. Scientists exposed a 1-year-old rat that was raised in a normal environment and had normal vision to only horizontal lines. Which of the following is the most reasonable prediction?

(A) After three weeks, the cells in the visual part of the rat's brain fail to respond to vertical lines.

(B) After six weeks, the cells in the visual part of the rat's brain fail to respond to vertical lines.

(C) After six weeks, the cells in the visual part of the rat's brain respond to vertical lines.

(D) After six months, the cells in the visual part of the rat's brain respond to vertical lines.

Study 8 shows that 6-month-old rats exposed to only horizontal lines for six months still have brain cells capable of responding to vertical lines. This info knocks out Choices (A) and (B). After six months, the wiring in the rat's visual part of the brain seems to be fixed, so you can assume that the 1-year-old rat's brain has fixed wiring.

Be careful of Choice (D). You can't say for sure what effects an exposure longer than six weeks will have. Choice (C) is a much safer (and correct!) choice.

TIP

Have you been noticing throughout these answer explanations how often you can narrow the answers down to two choices very quickly? If you're in a hurry or if you're confused, make a quick guess. Remember that the ACT doesn't penalize you for wrong answers.

8. Suppose the researchers subjected *R. norvegicus domestica* that were 6 weeks old at the beginning of the study to six weeks of complete darkness. Based on information in the table, the level of brain activity in response to horizontal stimuli that the researchers measured in these subjects at the end of the study was most likely:

(F) less than 5 percent

(G) between 5 percent and 60 percent

(H) between 60 percent and 75 percent

(J) greater than 75 percent

To answer this question, examine the results in the column that shows the brain response to horizonal stimuli for studies that exposed rats to complete darkness for six weeks, Study 3 and Study 6. The newborn rats in Study 3 displayed 5 percent activity when exposed to horizontal stimuli, and the 6-month-old rats in Study 6 displayed 50 percent activity when exposed to horizontal stimuli. This comparison indicates that rats that were older at the beginning of the study responded better to horizontal stimuli than the newborn subjects.

Therefore, there is no reason to believe that rats that were 6 weeks old at the beginning of the study would show less brain activity than the newborns, so Choice (F) is incorrect. Nor does the table suggest any reason to believe that the younger rats would register a higher percentage of brain activity in response to horizontal activity than the older rats in Study 6. Therefore, Choices (H) and (J) must be wrong. The rats in the new study most likely had brain activity that measured above the 5 percent indicated for newborns, most likely closer to the 50 percent indicated for the older rats in Study 6. So the correct answer is Choice (G).

9. Which study best shows or studies best show that a particular environmental stimulus can lead to a change in the way the cells in the visual part of a rat's brain respond?

(A) Study 4 only

(B) Study 4 and Study 5 only

(C) Study 5 and Study 8 only

(D) Study 1, Study 5, and Study 8 only

First, notice that the answer choices only concern Studies, 1, 4, 5, and 8. Don't waste time evaluating Studies 2, 3, and 7.

Study 1 was performed with newborn rat pups that received a variety of stimuli and weren't subjected to complete darkness. Because this study didn't isolate one particular controlled environmental stimulation, it doesn't best indicate how one environmental component affects the brain. You can eliminate Choice (D).

Study 4 looks good. It isolates one controlled environmental stimulus. Exposure to only vertical lines caused a loss of cells able to respond to horizontal lines and a gain of cells able to respond to vertical lines. Because the correct answer must have Study 4 in it, eliminate Choice (C).

Study 5 is very similar to Study 4 in that it tests what happens to the rats when exposed to just one controlled stimulus. Study 5 shows a loss of cells able to respond to vertical lines and a gain of cells able to respond to horizontal lines. So the correct answer is Choice (B).

Notice that by using process of elimination you can avoid examining Study 8 altogether. What a fantastic time-saver! If you want to be absolutely sure, go ahead and verify that Study 8 doesn't work. Study 8 shows that the controlled environment for 6-month-old rats didn't alter their brain activity or ability to navigate horizontal and vertical obstacles. Their results were the same as those for newborn and 6-week-old rats that received a variety of stimuli. This study, taken by itself, suggests little support for an environmental contribution.

10. If Study 4 is conducted but Studies 3 and 5 are not, can the scientists conclude that all cells in the visual part of a rat pup's brain require stimulation in order to function?

   (F) Yes, because Studies 3 and 5 test what happens when brain cells are not exposed to vertical lines.

   (G) Yes, because Study 4 tests both vertical and horizontal-responding cells.

   (H) No, because Study 4 only tests whether brain cells respond to vertical lines.

   (J) No, because Study 4 does not test whether vertical-responding cells require stimulation.

This "yes, yes, no, no" question tests whether you understand that experimental results are limited when only certain conditions are tested. Notice that the answer choices indicate that you're focusing on whether the studies tested responses to horizontal and vertical lines. Eliminate Choices (G) and (H) because they're not true. Study 4 didn't test responses to vertical lines.

Choices (F) and (J) provide true statements, but only Choice (J) pinpoints the limitations of Study 4 — that it doesn't test vertical-responding cells. Studies 3 and 5 did test the vertical factor and allow for a more general conclusion regarding brain cells and environmental input, so they're necessary to understand the role of all cells. So the answer has to be Choice (J). Study 4 is inadequate by itself.

11. On the basis of all the studies, which of the following best summarizes the role of the environment in the development of a rat's visual brain-cell responses?

   (A) The environment has no effect on the development of a rat's visual brain-cell responses.

   (B) Environmental input early in a rat's life contributes to the continuation of normal brain-cell responses to stimuli.

   (C) Environmental input can change the pattern of brain-cell responses throughout a rat's life.

   (D) The environment is the only factor that influences brain-cell responses.

If Choice (A) were true, the pups in Studies 3, 4, and 5 would have normal visual responses. Eliminate Choice (A). If Choice (C) were true, the rats in Studies 6, 7, and 8 would show a change in response patterns. Choice (D) is at odds with Study 1. If the environment is the only factor, why do newborn rats show responses to all types of stimuli? This reasoning leaves only Choice (B), which is correct.

TIP

Are you noticing and using the wording in the questions and choices to help you choose and eliminate answers? The conservative language ("contributes to the continuation" rather than "directly determines") reinforces Choice (B) as the answer. Notice how easily you can contradict Choice (A), which contains the word *no*, Choice (C), which says *throughout*, and Choice (D), which includes *only*.

12. Which of the following studies would probably add the most new information to the work done in this set of experiments?

(F) A study identical to Study 3, except that the pups are in the dark environment for seven weeks.

(G) A study identical to Study 6, except that the rats are in the dark environment for five weeks.

(H) A study identical to Study 6, except that the study uses 1-year-old rats.

(J) A study identical to Studies 4 and 5, except that the rats are exposed only to diagonal lines.

Study 3 shows that six weeks of darkness almost entirely wipes out the cells' ability to respond. Perhaps seven weeks would cause a complete cessation of responding, but the point made from Study 3 (namely, that lack of visual stimulation leads to impaired brain-cell responding) has already been established. Therefore, the study mentioned in Choice (F) won't add much.

Study 6 strongly suggests that the response patterns in the visual part of a rat's brain are fixed enough at six months so that six weeks of an abnormal environment have no noticeable effect. If six weeks have no noticeable effect, why would five weeks be any different? Eliminate Choice (G). If the brain-cell responses are fixed by the time a rat is 6 months old, you can reasonably expect that a 1-year-old rat would show the same responses. Eliminate Choice (H).

The study mentioned in Choice (J) would help because it would show what happens to cells that respond to lines that are oriented both vertically and horizontally. This study would add some information regarding how precise the brain cells are in regard to lines in the environment. For example, is a diagonal line close enough to a vertical line that the exposure only to diagonal lines still allows the rat to respond to vertical lines? The answer to this question may increase understanding of how the environment interacts with the visual part of a rat's brain.

Writing Practice Question

The prevailing attitude in many countries is that civic leaders must maintain the highest ethical and moral standards. Some people think that this attitude sets a good example for a country and its citizens. Others argue that leaders who show normal human flaws connect them with those they lead and thereby enable progress and growth. It is important to consider the role that ethical standards play in evaluating our leaders.

Read and carefully consider these perspectives. Each one suggests a particular way of thinking about the role of ethics in leadership.

Perspective 1: Why do we vote for our civic leaders if we want them to be just like everyone else? There are millions of people in this country, and we choose one to represent us all. Leaders should indeed be held to higher moral and ethical standards because all eyes, young and old, are on them at all times. We want the person in a position of power to be someone our children can look up to.

Perspective 2: People will be more likely to embrace and respect their political and civic leaders if they feel they are human and easy to identify with. Look at Bill Clinton — he clearly made errors and showed poor judgment, but is still one of the most beloved ex-presidents in our nation's history.

Perspective 3: If we do not hold our political and civic leaders to a higher standard, how are we supposed to garner the respect of other countries? For many nations, our leaders are all they know of America. We want to gain their respect and admiration, and the best starting point for doing so is electing individuals of strong moral and ethical stature.

Write a unified, coherent essay in which you evaluate multiple perspectives as to whether leaders should be held to higher moral and ethical standards than the general population. In your essay, be sure to do the following:

» Clearly state your own perspective on the issue and analyze the relationship between your perspective and at least one other perspective.

» Develop and support your ideas with reasoning and examples.

» Organize your ideas clearly and logically.

» Communicate your ideas effectively in standard written English.

Your perspective may be in full agreement with any of the others, in partial agreement, or wholly different.

In this prompt, you may argue for or against holding leaders to a higher moral and ethical standard than the common citizen. Say that you agree with the author of Perspective 1 that leaders should be more accountable for their actions than the average person. Your thesis paragraph may state that leaders are leaders for a reason — because they embody the ideals of a given population and because anyone could be a leader if leaders shared the same flaws as everyone else.

Your subsequent arguments may cite examples of elected officials whose poor or lack of judgment resulted in problems for those they governed. For example, you may mention a politician who misused his power or access to government funds to help further his own agenda. You may note that a leader is inherently in a position to serve as a role model and should, therefore, be expected to act accordingly at all times while in the public eye.

You may choose to address the opposing side offered by the author of Perspective 2 by stating that, while it's true that all humans are flawed by nature, leaders become leaders because of something exemplary about them. People elect and choose them because they aren't just like everyone else. Therefore, it's acceptable to hold them to a higher standard.

To wrap things up, your closing paragraph needs to echo, not directly repeat, the key points you make in the essay to support your initial argument and whether you agree with the perspectives given.

Should you choose to support the opposing side, you may formulate your thesis around the idea that great leaders are a representation of the population they rule, flaws and all. They were chosen for a leadership role based on their ability to relate and identify with the people they govern, and this ability enables them to effectively make decisions in the best interests of their people. Strengthen your argument with real-life examples, such as citing a politician whose moral character is undeniably questionable (like the Bill Clinton example provided in Perspective 2) and yet who is still revered as one of the best and most effective leaders of our time. Or offer a similar example of a leader whose questionable ethics didn't interfere with his or her ability to effectively rule a given population.

Providing inspirational examples of leaders who have been effective despite their character flaws has the added benefit of addressing the concerns of the opposition. You may point out that character flaws don't necessarily weaken a leader's accomplishments and may actually enhance the effectiveness of leaders who acknowledge their weaknesses. Perhaps leaders who are more representative of the common man may inspire others who work to overcome character flaws that they, too, may one day land a position of power and decision making. Plus, people are more likely to see flawed leaders as relatable, approachable figures who are more likely to have the general public's best interests at heart.

Conclude with a few lines that summarize the key arguments you make in your essay and draw a final conclusion as to why moral and ethical equals are the best choice for leadership roles.

Block **4**

Taking a (Shortened) Practice Test

Here's your chance to test what you know on an ACT sample test. The following exam consists of five tests: a 25-minute English Test, a 30-minute Mathematics Test, a 20-minute Reading Test, a 17-minute Science Test, and a 40-minute Writing Test. If you remember from Block 1 that these tests are actually twice as long, you're right! To help you prepare for the ACT in five hours or less, we shortened each test by about half. The exception is the writing test because there's only one prompt, and half a prompt won't do you much good.

This practice test offer representative example of the passages and questions you'll find on the full ACT.

To make sure you replicate the torturous climate of the real experience, take this test under the following normal exam conditions:

>> Sit where you won't be interrupted or tempted to use your cellphone or binge multiple seasons of your favorite shows.

>> Use the answer sheet provided to give you practice filling in the dots.

>> Set your timer for the time limits indicated at the beginning of each test in this exam.

>> Don't go on to the next test until the time allotted for the test you're taking is up.

>> Check your work for that test only; don't look at more than one test at a time.

>> Don't take a break during any test.

>> Give yourself one ten-minute break between the Math Test and the Reading Test.

TIP

When you finish this practice exam, you can check your answers using the answer key at the end of this block and read more detailed explanations of how to approach every question. Go through the answer explanations to all the questions, not just the ones that you missed. Intertwined in the explanations are reviews of important concepts from the previous blocks and tips for improving the efficiency of your approach.

Note: The ACT Writing Test is optional. If you register to take the Writing Test, you'll take it after you've completed the other four tests. If you're not registering for the Writing Test, you can skip the practice.

Answer Sheet

Begin with Number 1 for each new test.

English Test

1. Ⓐ Ⓑ Ⓒ Ⓓ	24. Ⓕ Ⓖ Ⓗ Ⓙ	
2. Ⓕ Ⓖ Ⓗ Ⓙ	25. Ⓐ Ⓑ Ⓒ Ⓓ	
3. Ⓐ Ⓑ Ⓒ Ⓓ	26. Ⓕ Ⓖ Ⓗ Ⓙ	
4. Ⓕ Ⓖ Ⓗ Ⓙ	27. Ⓐ Ⓑ Ⓒ Ⓓ	
5. Ⓐ Ⓑ Ⓒ Ⓓ	28. Ⓕ Ⓖ Ⓗ Ⓙ	
6. Ⓕ Ⓖ Ⓗ Ⓙ	29. Ⓐ Ⓑ Ⓒ Ⓓ	
7. Ⓐ Ⓑ Ⓒ Ⓓ	30. Ⓕ Ⓖ Ⓗ Ⓙ	
8. Ⓕ Ⓖ Ⓗ Ⓙ	31. Ⓐ Ⓑ Ⓒ Ⓓ	
9. Ⓐ Ⓑ Ⓒ Ⓓ	32. Ⓕ Ⓖ Ⓗ Ⓙ	
10. Ⓕ Ⓖ Ⓗ Ⓙ	33. Ⓐ Ⓑ Ⓒ Ⓓ	
11. Ⓐ Ⓑ Ⓒ Ⓓ	34. Ⓕ Ⓖ Ⓗ Ⓙ	
12. Ⓕ Ⓖ Ⓗ Ⓙ	35. Ⓐ Ⓑ Ⓒ Ⓓ	
13. Ⓐ Ⓑ Ⓒ Ⓓ	36. Ⓕ Ⓖ Ⓗ Ⓙ	
14. Ⓕ Ⓖ Ⓗ Ⓙ	37. Ⓐ Ⓑ Ⓒ Ⓓ	
15. Ⓐ Ⓑ Ⓒ Ⓓ	38. Ⓕ Ⓖ Ⓗ Ⓙ	
16. Ⓕ Ⓖ Ⓗ Ⓙ	39. Ⓐ Ⓑ Ⓒ Ⓓ	
17. Ⓐ Ⓑ Ⓒ Ⓓ	40. Ⓕ Ⓖ Ⓗ Ⓙ	
18. Ⓕ Ⓖ Ⓗ Ⓙ	41. Ⓐ Ⓑ Ⓒ Ⓓ	
19. Ⓐ Ⓑ Ⓒ Ⓓ	42. Ⓕ Ⓖ Ⓗ Ⓙ	
20. Ⓕ Ⓖ Ⓗ Ⓙ	43. Ⓐ Ⓑ Ⓒ Ⓓ	
21. Ⓐ Ⓑ Ⓒ Ⓓ	44. Ⓕ Ⓖ Ⓗ Ⓙ	
22. Ⓕ Ⓖ Ⓗ Ⓙ	45. Ⓐ Ⓑ Ⓒ Ⓓ	
23. Ⓐ Ⓑ Ⓒ Ⓓ		

Mathematics Test

1. Ⓐ Ⓑ Ⓒ Ⓓ Ⓔ	16. Ⓕ Ⓖ Ⓗ Ⓙ Ⓚ
2. Ⓕ Ⓖ Ⓗ Ⓙ Ⓚ	17. Ⓐ Ⓑ Ⓒ Ⓓ Ⓔ
3. Ⓐ Ⓑ Ⓒ Ⓓ Ⓔ	18. Ⓕ Ⓖ Ⓗ Ⓙ Ⓚ
4. Ⓕ Ⓖ Ⓗ Ⓙ Ⓚ	19. Ⓐ Ⓑ Ⓒ Ⓓ Ⓔ
5. Ⓐ Ⓑ Ⓒ Ⓓ Ⓔ	20. Ⓕ Ⓖ Ⓗ Ⓙ Ⓚ
6. Ⓕ Ⓖ Ⓗ Ⓙ Ⓚ	21. Ⓐ Ⓑ Ⓒ Ⓓ Ⓔ
7. Ⓐ Ⓑ Ⓒ Ⓓ Ⓔ	22. Ⓕ Ⓖ Ⓗ Ⓙ Ⓚ
8. Ⓕ Ⓖ Ⓗ Ⓙ Ⓚ	23. Ⓐ Ⓑ Ⓒ Ⓓ Ⓔ
9. Ⓐ Ⓑ Ⓒ Ⓓ Ⓔ	24. Ⓕ Ⓖ Ⓗ Ⓙ Ⓚ
10. Ⓕ Ⓖ Ⓗ Ⓙ Ⓚ	25. Ⓐ Ⓑ Ⓒ Ⓓ Ⓔ
11. Ⓐ Ⓑ Ⓒ Ⓓ Ⓔ	26. Ⓕ Ⓖ Ⓗ Ⓙ Ⓚ
12. Ⓕ Ⓖ Ⓗ Ⓙ Ⓚ	27. Ⓐ Ⓑ Ⓒ Ⓓ Ⓔ
13. Ⓐ Ⓑ Ⓒ Ⓓ Ⓔ	28. Ⓕ Ⓖ Ⓗ Ⓙ Ⓚ
14. Ⓕ Ⓖ Ⓗ Ⓙ Ⓚ	29. Ⓐ Ⓑ Ⓒ Ⓓ Ⓔ
15. Ⓐ Ⓑ Ⓒ Ⓓ Ⓔ	30. Ⓕ Ⓖ Ⓗ Ⓙ Ⓚ

Reading Test	Science Test
1. Ⓐ Ⓑ Ⓒ Ⓓ	1. Ⓐ Ⓑ Ⓒ Ⓓ
2. Ⓕ Ⓖ Ⓗ Ⓙ	2. Ⓕ Ⓖ Ⓗ Ⓙ
3. Ⓐ Ⓑ Ⓒ Ⓓ	3. Ⓐ Ⓑ Ⓒ Ⓓ
4. Ⓕ Ⓖ Ⓗ Ⓙ	4. Ⓕ Ⓖ Ⓗ Ⓙ
5. Ⓐ Ⓑ Ⓒ Ⓓ	5. Ⓐ Ⓑ Ⓒ Ⓓ
6. Ⓕ Ⓖ Ⓗ Ⓙ	6. Ⓕ Ⓖ Ⓗ Ⓙ
7. Ⓐ Ⓑ Ⓒ Ⓓ	7. Ⓐ Ⓑ Ⓒ Ⓓ
8. Ⓕ Ⓖ Ⓗ Ⓙ	8. Ⓕ Ⓖ Ⓗ Ⓙ
9. Ⓐ Ⓑ Ⓒ Ⓓ	9. Ⓐ Ⓑ Ⓒ Ⓓ
10. Ⓕ Ⓖ Ⓗ Ⓙ	10. Ⓕ Ⓖ Ⓗ Ⓙ
11. Ⓐ Ⓑ Ⓒ Ⓓ	11. Ⓐ Ⓑ Ⓒ Ⓓ
12. Ⓕ Ⓖ Ⓗ Ⓙ	12. Ⓕ Ⓖ Ⓗ Ⓙ
13. Ⓐ Ⓑ Ⓒ Ⓓ	13. Ⓐ Ⓑ Ⓒ Ⓓ
14. Ⓕ Ⓖ Ⓗ Ⓙ	14. Ⓕ Ⓖ Ⓗ Ⓙ
15. Ⓐ Ⓑ Ⓒ Ⓓ	15. Ⓐ Ⓑ Ⓒ Ⓓ
16. Ⓕ Ⓖ Ⓗ Ⓙ	16. Ⓕ Ⓖ Ⓗ Ⓙ
17. Ⓐ Ⓑ Ⓒ Ⓓ	17. Ⓐ Ⓑ Ⓒ Ⓓ
18. Ⓕ Ⓖ Ⓗ Ⓙ	18. Ⓕ Ⓖ Ⓗ Ⓙ
19. Ⓐ Ⓑ Ⓒ Ⓓ	19. Ⓐ Ⓑ Ⓒ Ⓓ
20. Ⓕ Ⓖ Ⓗ Ⓙ	20. Ⓕ Ⓖ Ⓗ Ⓙ

English Test

TIME: 25 minutes for 45 questions

DIRECTIONS: Following are three passages with underlined portions. Alternate ways of stating the underlined portions come after the passages. Choose the best alternative; if the original is the best way of stating the underlined portion, choose NO CHANGE.

The test also has questions that refer to the passages or ask you to reorder the sentences within the passages. These questions are identified by a number in a box. Choose the best answer and shade in the corresponding oval on your answer sheet.

Passage 1

Personal Trainers Help Drop Pounds

When it comes to losing weight fast; some methods are more effective than others. For those who are serious about slimming down in a short amount of time, one of the easiest ways being to hire a personal trainer.

Because there's no standard of licensure for the profession, it's critical that you do your homework prior to hiring one. 5 Seek out a certified fitness professional — ideally, someone who is capable and able to communicate well and clearly. You also may want to pick someone whose physique mirrors one that you would have wanted for yourself. For example, if you're inspired by your trainer, you're more likely to stay on track and less likely to skip out on workout sessions.

It's also a good idea to select someone with whom you connect, at least to some extent, on a personal level. Not all personalities mesh well together. Some people thrive off positive reinforcement, others fare better when faced with constructive criticism. 12

To decide, whether a potential trainer will be a good fit, ask questions about training style and fitness philosophy. Weight loss and physical fitness starts with effective training methods, and a personal trainer can be the perfect person to get you on track toward a new and better you. 15

1. **(A)** NO CHANGE
   (B) losing weight fast, some methods are
   (C) losing weight fast: some methods are
   (D) losing weight fast — some methods are

2. **(F)** NO CHANGE
   (G) one of the easiest ways to be
   (H) one of the easiest ways is
   (J) the easiest way being

3. **(A)** NO CHANGE
   (B) profession, its critical
   (C) profession, its' critical
   (D) profession; it's critical

4. **(F)** NO CHANGE
   (G) them
   (H) a coach
   (J) it

5. At this point, the author is considering adding the following statement:

This might include asking friends, family, or co-workers, or reading online reviews or testimonials.

Should the writer make this addition here?

(A) Yes, because it provides specific ways the reader may accomplish the prior suggestion offered in the passage.

(B) Yes, because it further explains the benefits of using a personal trainer.

(C) No, because it contains information that has been stated previously in the passage.

(D) No, because it does not emphasize how easy it is to find a personal trainer.

6. Which of the following alternatives to the underlined portion is LEAST acceptable?

(F) competent

(G) useful

(H) experienced

(J) skilled

7. (A) NO CHANGE

(B) clearly

(C) well and clear

(D) in a clear manner

8. (F) NO CHANGE

(G) want

(H) wanted

(J) had wanted

9. (A) NO CHANGE

(B) However,

(C) To illustrate,

(D) Delete the underlined portion and capitalize if.

10. Which of the following choices best guides the reader from the preceding paragraph and introduces this new paragraph?

(F) NO CHANGE

(G) Always check a trainer's credentials before you sign on.

(H) Some trainers offer better gym facilities than others.

(J) Missing workout sessions may cause you to give up on your training altogether.

11. (A) NO CHANGE

(B) reinforcement, others fare best

(C) reinforcement, but others fare better

(D) reinforcement, and, others fare best

12. Which of the following sentences, if added here, would most effectively conclude this paragraph and introduce the topic of the next?

(F) Trainers who may seem tough at first are eventually the most effective.

(G) If you don't like your trainer, you're unlikely to be happy with your results.

(H) Finding a trainer whose teaching style meshes with your learning style will likely give you the best results.

(J) Similarly, when you like the taste of healthy foods, you're more likely to eat them

13. (A) NO CHANGE

(B) To decide whether a potential trainer will be a good fit,

(C) To decide whether, a potential trainer, will be a good fit

(D) To decide whether a potential trainer, will be a good fit,

14. (F) NO CHANGE

(G) begins

(H) starting

(J) start

GO ON TO NEXT PAGE

15. Suppose the author's intent was to create an essay that highlights some of the best ways to lose weight. Would this essay successfully achieve that goal?

   (A) Yes, because the essay shows that hiring a trainer is a helpful way to lose weight.

   (B) Yes, because the essay highlights the importance of creating and sticking to a workout regimen.

   (C) No, because the essay does not reveal that hiring a trainer may actually lead to weight gain from increased muscle mass.

   (D) No, because the essay focuses on only one method for losing weight.

Passage 2

The Pitching Machine

[1]

Known as Americans pastime, and to many
                  16   17
baseball means much more. Hitting baseballs is a major part of many a childhood and using a
                                       18
pitching machine can be a great resource for ball players at any level to fine-tune their skills behind
                                               19
the plate.

[2]

Among the more popular pitching machine models are circular-wheel machines and arm-action machines. If you're looking to buy one, look for a variety that closely simulates the pitches
                              20
you'll experience during real game play. You should also look for a machine that simulates an assortment of different release points. Machines that have thrown an array of different pitches
          21
allow players to work on hitting while
improving hand-eye coordination.
          22

[3]

When choosing a machine, take into account the age of the player. 23 Players who are just starting out will likely benefit most from a pitching machine that releases balls slower, allowing the
                                        24
players to familiarize themselves with the basics of batting.

[4]

More advanced players who hit at more
                          25
elevated levels may favor a fast-pitch machine. Featuring many customizable options, a hitter can
adjust the amount of time that passes between the
                                    26
release of each baseball and set the machines at
different heights.

[5]

Baseball is a wonderful sport to take part in,
                                      27
and these pitching machines can prove tremen-dously effective for players of all skill levels. 28 The device is a home run for players who
want to and are interested in maximizing their
                                    29
skills at the plate. 30

16. (F) NO CHANGE
   (G) America's pastime
   (H) the pastime of American's
   (J) Americas pastime

17. (A) NO CHANGE
   (B) but, to many, baseball
   (C) to many baseball
   (D) DELETE the underlined portion.

18. (F) NO CHANGE
   (G) childhood. Therefore, using
   (H) childhood, but using
   (J) childhood, using

19. (A) NO CHANGE
    (B) they're
    (C) there
    (D) its

20. Which of the following alternatives to the underlined portion is LEAST acceptable?
    (F) copies
    (G) mimics
    (H) imitates
    (J) fakes

21. (A) NO CHANGE
    (B) throw
    (C) throwing
    (D) threw

22. (F) NO CHANGE
    (G) improving hand-eye coordination at the same time
    (H) also improving hand-eye coordination
    (J) improving, at the same time, hand-eye coordination

23. The author is considering adding the following phrase to the end of the preceding sentence:

    to improve safety and maximize the effectiveness of the machine.

    Should the writer make this addition here?

    (A) Yes, because it clarifies the reasons for selecting a particular type of pitching machine.
    (B) Yes, because it implies that younger players may not experience the same benefits from pitching machines as older players.
    (C) No, because it distracts the reader from the main topic of the paragraph.
    (D) No, because it repeats a point made earlier in the essay.

24. (F) NO CHANGE
    (G) more slow
    (H) more slowly
    (J) more slower

25. (A) NO CHANGE
    (B) who hit at elevated levels
    (C) hitting at elevated levels
    (D) DELETE the underlined portion.

26. (F) NO CHANGE
    (G) adjustments may be made to the amount of time that passes between the release of each baseball and the machines' height settings.
    (H) time between baseballs may be adjusted and heights changed.
    (J) the machines may be adjusted to change their height and the amount of time that passes between the release of each baseball.

27. Which of the following is LEAST acceptable?
    (A) NO CHANGE
    (B) in which to take part
    (C) of which to take part
    (D) DELETE the underlined portion.

28. The writer is considering adding a comma and the following point after "levels" in the preceding sentence: but mostly for younger hitters

    Should the writer make this addition?

    (F) No, because it contradicts the author's point that pitching machines are equally effective for players of all skill levels.
    (G) No, because professional players likely benefit more from pitching machines than do little league players.
    (H) Yes, because it furthers the author's argument that young players benefit more from pitching machines than older ones.
    (J) Yes, because it builds upon the point made in the fourth paragraph.

29. (A) NO CHANGE
    (B) have an interest and desire in maximizing
    (C) want to maximize
    (D) aspire and endeavor to maximize

GO ON TO NEXT PAGE

30. For the sake of logic and coherence, Paragraph 5 should be placed:

    (F) where it is now.

    (G) before Paragraph 1.

    (H) after Paragraph 2.

    (J) after Paragraph 3.

Passage 3

Teddy Roosevelt: A Political Maverick

No figure better represents the Progressive Era than Theodore "Teddy" Roosevelt. Born into a wealthy New York family, Roosevelt has risen to
<u>has risen</u>
31
national prominence rather quickly. Early in his
<u>prominence</u>
32
career, Roosevelt served as commissioner of the New York City Police Department before becoming the Assistant Secretary of the Navy. In the Spanish-American War, Roosevelt gained notoriety for leading his military volunteer unit, the "Rough Riders" to victory in the Battle of San Juan Hill in
<u>the "Rough</u>
<u>Riders" to victory in the Battle of San Juan Hill</u>
33
Cuba. In 1900, Roosevelt became Republican William McKinley's vice-presidential candidate. McKinley was assassinated in 1901. [34] Roosevelt became the most youngest President of the United
<u>most youngest</u>
35
States at age 42.

"TR," as he came to be known, exuded an
<u>exuded</u>
36
active, vibrant personality. Roosevelt was intelligent, well read, and knows a great deal about the
<u>knows a great deal</u>
37
environment, history, and naval strategy. He demonstrated his love for sports and competition by participating in boxing, being a big-game hunter,
<u>being a big-game hunter</u>
38
and other outdoor pursuits. His dynamic lifestyle carried over into his presidency, which lasted from 1901 to 1909, and he became one of the most active
<u>most active</u>
39
<u>and busy</u> presidents in the history of the

United States. Among the topics he tackled were
<u>Among the topics he tackled were</u>
40
trusts, railroads, safety in the food industry, and the environment.

Roosevelt demonstrated his distaste for trusts during the coal strike crisis of 1902. No fewer than 50,000 coal miners went on strike, demanding better working conditions and higher pay. Roosevelt intervened, inviting the union representatives and mine owners to the White House to try to find a solution. Therefore, the owners refused to speak
<u>Therefore,</u>
41
with the union representatives. Roosevelt was infuriated by this rebuff, and he threatened to send federal troops to operate the mines. At the urging of J.P. Morgan (the renowned financier who formed the U.S. Steel Corporation), the owners backed down and gave the miners shorter workdays (9 hours) and better wages (10% wage increases). [42]

Railroad reform was another of Roosevelt's important contributions to the progressive cause. During the beginning of the 20th century, railroad
<u>During</u>
43
companies controlled the prices of their services. Roosevelt believed that this system gave private companies too much power, which ultimately hurt consumers. For example, he supported the
<u>For example,</u>
44
Hepburn Railroad Act, which gave the Interstate Commerce Commission the power to regulate the prices of railroad rates and audit railroad company's financial records. Congress passed the
<u>company's</u>
45
Hepburn Railroad Act, and Roosevelt signed it into law in 1906. Roosevelt proved that he would not hesitate to challenge the powers and abuses of big business.

31. (A) NO CHANGE
    (B) rises
    (C) rose
    (D) has rose

32. (F) NO CHANGE
    (G) infamy
    (H) obscurity
    (J) anonymity

33. (A) NO CHANGE
    (B) the "Rough Riders," to victory in the Battle of San Juan Hill
    (C) the "Rough Riders" to victory, in the Battle of San Juan Hill
    (D) the "Rough Riders," to victory in the Battle of San Juan Hill,

34. The author is considering inserting a few lines about what led to McKinley's assassination and who was responsible. Would that insertion be appropriate here?

    (F) Yes, because it would clarify how Roosevelt came to assume the presidency.
    (G) Yes, because it contains important clarifying information about McKinley.
    (H) No, because the focus of the passage is Roosevelt, not McKinley.
    (J) No, because this information should appear earlier in the passage.

35. (A) NO CHANGE
    (B) younger
    (C) most young
    (D) youngest

36. Which of the following substitutes for the underlined word would be the LEAST appropriate?

    (F) infused
    (G) conveyed
    (H) radiated
    (J) emanated

37. (A) NO CHANGE
    (B) had known quite a bit
    (C) knowledgeable
    (D) he knew

38. (F) NO CHANGE
    (G) was a big-game hunter
    (H) engaging in big-game hunting
    (J) big-game hunting

39. (A) NO CHANGE
    (B) most active
    (C) most active and lively
    (D) DELETE the underlined portion.

40. (F) NO CHANGE
    (G) Among the topics that were tackled were trusts,
    (H) Among the tackled topics was trusts,
    (J) Trusts were among the tackled topics along with

41. (A) NO CHANGE
    (B) However,
    (C) Finally,
    (D) As a result,

42. The author is considering deleting the preceding sentence. Without the sentence, the paragraph would primarily lose:

    (F) details that summarize one of Roosevelt's specific accomplishments.
    (G) interesting but irrelevant information.
    (H) foreshadowing of an event detailed in the next paragraph.
    (J) general observations about Roosevelt's achievements.

43. (A) NO CHANGE
    (B) At
    (C) After
    (D) Through

44. (F) NO CHANGE
    (G) Nevertheless,
    (H) On the contrary,
    (J) Thus,

45. (A) NO CHANGE
    (B) companies
    (C) companies'
    (D) companys'

Mathematics Test

TIME: 30 minutes for 30 questions

DIRECTIONS: Each question has five answer choices. Choose the best answer for each question and shade the corresponding oval on your answer sheet.

1. What is the value of $y \times 2^x$ if $x = 3$ and $y = 2$?

(A) 8

(B) 16

(C) 12

(D) 10

(E) 64

2. The first four terms of a geometric sequence are .75, 1.5, 3, and 6. What is the fifth term?

(F) 12

(G) 9

(H) 18

(J) 11.25

(K) 36

3. In the following figure, A, B, and C are collinear. The measure of $\angle ABD$ is three times that of $\angle DBC$. What is the measure of $\angle ABD$?

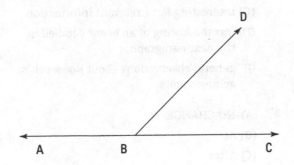

(A) 135°

(B) 120°

(C) 67.5°

(D) 60°

(E) 45°

4. Which of the following is equivalent to $\dfrac{3}{\frac{3}{8}}$?

(F) 3

(G) 24

(H) $\dfrac{9}{8}$

(J) $\dfrac{1}{8}$

(K) 8

5. What is the measure of angle b in the following figure where lines C and D are parallel?

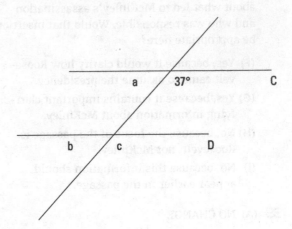

(A) 37°

(B) 53°

(C) 127°

(D) 143°

(E) 180°

6. Ross has 2 black socks and 2 white socks lying in his drawer. If he blindly selects 2 socks from the drawer, what is the chance that he will select the black pair?

(F) $\frac{1}{6}$

(G) $\frac{1}{4}$

(H) $\frac{1}{2}$

(J) $\frac{5}{6}$

(K) $\frac{3}{4}$

7. A triangular ramp from the ground to the bed of a truck that stands 6 feet off the ground has a base of 8 feet. How long in feet is the length of the bottom of the ramp?

(A) 5 feet

(B) 5.29 feet

(C) 8 feet

(D) 10 feet

(E) 100 feet

8. What is the solution to $\frac{1}{6}+\frac{1}{2}+\frac{1}{3}$?

(F) $\frac{1}{11}$

(G) $\frac{3}{11}$

(H) $\frac{1}{2}$

(J) 1

(K) $\frac{37}{36}$

9. Which is the correct factoring of $4x^2-4x-3$?

(A) $(2x-1)(2x+3)$

(B) $(4x+1)(x-3)$

(C) $(2x+1)(2x-3)$

(D) $(4x-1)(x+3)$

(E) $(4x-1)(4x+3)$

10. At what point does $7x+4y=28$ intersect the y-axis in the standard (x, y) coordinate plane?

(F) $(4, 0)$

(G) $(7, 0)$

(H) $(0, 4)$

(J) $(0, 7)$

(K) $(28, 0)$

11. Simplify $\left(\frac{3x}{y}\right)\left(\frac{x^3y^2}{6}\right)$.

(A) $\frac{x^4y}{2}$

(B) $\frac{x^4y^3}{2}$

(C) $\frac{x^2y^3}{2}$

(D) $\frac{3x+x^3y^2}{y+6}$

(E) $\frac{3x+x^3y^2}{6y}$

12. Jacob is making cupcakes for his friend Jack's birthday party. The only supplies he needs to buy are x pounds of flour at $3.50 per pound, s pounds of sugar at $4.50 per pound, and 3 cupcake pans at $6 per pan. Which of the following expresses Jacob's total cost, in dollars, of providing the cupcakes for Jack's birthday party?

(A) $(x+\$3.50)(s+\$4.50)+\$18.00$

(B) $x+\$3.50+s+\$4.50+\$18.00$

(C) $\$3.50x+\$4.50s+\$18.00$

(D) $\$3.50s+\$4.50x+\$6.00$

(E) $(\$3.50x)(\$4.50s)+\$18.00$

13. What is the value of y in the following system of equations?

$2x+3y=6$

$x-y=8$

(A) 6

(B) 2

(C) 0

(D) −6

(E) −2

14. Which of the following is equal to 1.54×10^{-3}?

(A) 1,540

(B) 154

(C) 0.0154

(D) 0.00154

(E) 0.000154

GO ON TO NEXT PAGE

15. Tickets to a movie cost $8 for adults and $5 for children. If 40 tickets are sold for a total of $251, how many adult tickets were sold?

(A) 15

(B) 17

(C) 20

(D) 23

(E) 25

16. Which of the following functions is represented on the standard (x, y) coordinate plane shown here?

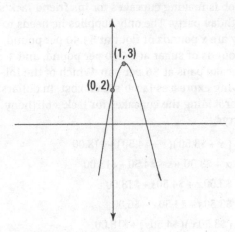

(F) $y = (x+3)^2 - 1$

(G) $y = -(x+3)^2 + 1$

(H) $y = -(x+1)^2 + 3$

(J) $y = (x-1)^2 + 3$

(K) $y = -(x-1)^2 + 3$

17. Which of the following represents the possible x-solutions to the inequality $4x - 5 < 9x + 2$?

(A) $x < -\dfrac{7}{5}$

(B) $x > -\dfrac{7}{5}$

(C) $x < \dfrac{7}{5}$

(D) $x > \dfrac{7}{5}$

(E) $x > \dfrac{9}{4}$

18. Which of the following could be the equation of line m graphed in the standard (x, y) coordinate plane shown here?

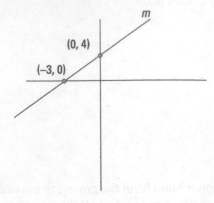

(F) $3x - 4y = 12$

(G) $4x - 3y = 12$

(H) $4y - 3x = 12$

(J) $3y - 4x = 12$

(K) $3y + 4x = 12$

19. Which of the following values for x makes $\log_6 9 + \log_6 x = 2$?

(A) $\dfrac{1}{3}$

(B) $1\dfrac{1}{3}$

(C) 3

(D) 4

(E) 27

20. What is the volume in cm^3 of a circular cylindrical soda can whose diameter is 10 cm and height is 15 cm?

(F) 10π

(G) 150π

(H) 375π

(J) 625π

(K) $15,000\pi$

21. If in the standard (x, y) coordinate plane the quadrilateral ABCD shown here were reflected over the line $y = 2$ to form quadrilateral $A_1B_1C_1D_1$, at what pair of coordinates would point A_1 lie?

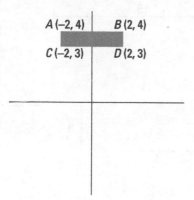

$A(-2, 4)$ $B(2, 4)$

$C(-2, 3)$ $D(2, 3)$

(A) $(-2, 0)$

(B) $(6, 4)$

(C) $(2, 4)$

(D) $(-2, -4)$

(E) $(-2, 2)$

22. Which of the following expresses all values of x that make the solution of $x^2 + x - 20$ positive and nonzero?

(F) $x > 20$

(G) $-5 < x < 4$

(H) $x > 20$ and $x < 0$

(J) $x - 5$ and $x4$

(K) $x > 4$

23. Klaus decided to give 20% of the money he got for his birthday to his favorite charity and put the rest in the bank. If he put $280 in the bank, how much money did he receive for his birthday?

(A) $56

(B) $70

(C) $350

(D) $336

(E) $375

24. If it costs $50 to fill up a 20-gallon tank of gas, how much would it cost to fill up a 16-gallon tank of gas?

(F) $37.50

(G) $62.50

(H) $46

(J) $48

(K) $40

25. In the right triangle shown here, what is cos C?

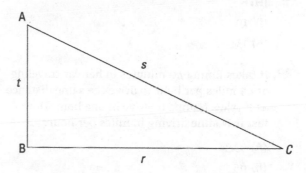

(A) $\dfrac{t}{r}$

(B) $\dfrac{s}{r}$

(C) $\dfrac{t}{s}$

(D) $\dfrac{r}{s}$

(E) $\dfrac{s}{t}$

26. What coordinate point is the midpoint of the line segment that goes from point $(-1, 3)$ to point $(5, -5)$ in the standard (x, y) coordinate plane?

(F) $(-3, 4)$

(G) $(2, -1)$

(H) $(3, -1)$

(J) $(2, 4)$

(K) $(-1, -5)$

27. For all pairs of real numbers x and y where $x = 3y + 8$, what does y equal?

(A) $\dfrac{x}{3} - 8$

(B) $x - \dfrac{8}{3}$

(C) $3y + 8$

(D) $\dfrac{x - 8}{3}$

(E) $x - 8$

GO ON TO NEXT PAGE

28. On the following number line, the distance between *A* and *D* is 28 units. The distance between *A* and *C* is 15 units. The distance between *B* and *D* is 18 units. What is the distance in units between *B* and *C*?

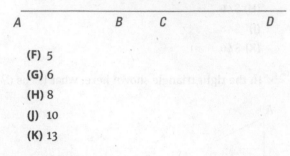

   A   *B*   *C*   *D*

(F) 5

(G) 6

(H) 8

(J) 10

(K) 13

29. It takes Emma 40 minutes in her car traveling at 45 miles per hour to drive the same distance as it takes Nadine to drive in one hour. How fast is Nadine driving in miles per hour?

(A) 53.3

(B) 65

(C) 30

(D) 67.5

(E) 35

30. What is the perimeter of the following polygon whose angles each measure 90°?

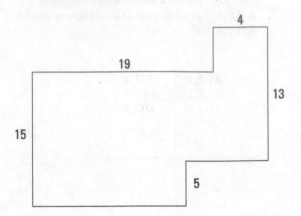

(F) 56

(G) 74

(H) 77

(J) 79

(K) 82

Reading Test

TIME: 20 minutes for 20 questions

DIRECTIONS: Each of the four passages in this section is followed by multiple questions. Answer each question based on what is stated or implied in the passage and shade the corresponding oval on your answer sheet.

Passage I — Prose Fiction

This passage is adapted from the novel, *Song of the Lark*, by Willa Sibert Cather.

Line

"And it was Summer, beautiful Summer!" Those were the words of Thea's favorite fairy tale, and she thought of them as she ran one Saturday morning in May, her music book under her arm.
(05) She was going to the Kohlers' to take her lesson, but she was in no hurry.

It was in the summer that one really lived. Then all the little overcrowded houses were opened wide, and the wind blew through them with sweet, earthy
(10) smells of garden-planting. People were out painting their fences. The cottonwood trees were a-flicker with sticky, yellow little leaves, and the feathery tamarisks were in pink bud. With the warm weather came freedom for everybody. The very old people,
(15) whom one had not seen all winter, came out and sunned themselves in the yard. The double windows were taken off the houses, the tormenting flannels in which children had been encased all winter were put away in boxes, and the youngsters felt a plea-
(20) sure in the cool cotton things next their skin.

Thea had to walk more than a mile to reach the Kohlers' house. On a little rise of ground that faced the open sandy plain, was the Kohlers' house, where Professor Wunsch lived. Fritz Kohler was the
(25) town tailor, one of the first settlers. He had moved there, built a little house and made a garden, when Moonstone was first marked down on the map. He had three sons, but they now worked on the railroad and were stationed in distant cities. One of
(30) them had gone to work for the Santa Fe, and lived in New Mexico.

Mrs. Kohler seldom crossed the ravine and went into the town except at Christmastime, when she had to buy presents to send to her old friends
(35) in Freeport, Illinois. As she did not go to church, she did not possess such a thing as a hat. Year after year she wore the same red hood in winter and a black sunbonnet in summer. She made her own dresses; the skirts came barely to her shoe-tops,
(40) and were gathered as full as they could possibly be

to the waistband. She preferred men's shoes, and usually wore the cast-offs of one of her sons. She had never learned much English, and her plants and shrubs were her companions. She lived for her men and her garden. Beside that sand gulch, she (45) had tried to reproduce a bit of her own village in the Rhine Valley. She hid herself behind the growth she had fostered, lived under the shade of what she had planted and watered and pruned. Shade, shade; that was what she was always planning and (50) making. Behind the high tamarisk hedge, her garden was a jungle of verdure in summer. Above the cherry trees and peach trees stood the windmill, which kept all this verdure alive. Outside, the sagebrush grew up to the very edge of the garden. (55)

Everyone in Moonstone was astonished when the Kohlers took in the wandering music-teacher. In seventeen years old Fritz had never had a crony, except the harness-maker and Spanish Johnny. This Wunsch came from God knew where, and (60) played in the dance orchestra, tuned pianos, and gave lessons. When Mrs. Kohler rescued him, he was sleeping in a dirty, unfurnished room over one of the saloons, and he had only two shirts in the world. Once he was under her roof, the old woman (65) went at him as she did at her garden. She sewed and washed and mended, and made him so clean and respectable that he was able to get a large class of pupils and rent a piano. As soon as he had money, he sent to the Narrow Gauge lodging-house, (70) in Denver, for a trunkful of music which had been held there for unpaid board. With tears in his eyes the old man—he was not over fifty, but sadly battered—told Mrs. Kohler that he asked nothing better of God than to end his days with her, and (75) to be buried in the garden, under her linden trees. They were not American basswood, but the European linden, which has honey-colored blooms in summer, with a fragrance that surpasses all trees and flowers and drives young people wild with joy. (80)

Thea was reflecting as she walked along that had it not been for Professor Wunsch she might have lived on for years without ever knowing the Kohlers, without ever seeing their garden or the inside of their house. (85)

GO ON TO NEXT PAGE →

Professor Wunsch went to the houses of his other pupils to give them their lessons, but one morning he told Mrs. Kronborg that Thea had talent. Mrs. Kronborg was a strange woman. That
(90) word "talent," which no one else in Moonstone would have understood, she comprehended perfectly. To any other woman, it would have meant that a child must have her hair curled every day and must play in public. Mrs. Kronborg knew it
(95) meant that Thea must practice four hours a day. A child with talent must be kept at the piano, just as a child with measles must be kept under the blankets.

1. Which of the following examples best parallels the analogy that Mrs. Kronborg made in the final paragraph?

   (A) A student with good writing skills must work harder on math.

   (B) A young girl with beauty must be kept under close watch.

   (C) A person with outdoor allergies must be kept indoors.

   (D) A child with learning differences may benefit from tutoring.

2. The author associates all of the following with the onset of summer EXCEPT:

   (F) seeing new neighbors

   (G) the blossoming of cottonwood trees

   (H) home dwellers painting their fences

   (J) children wearing cool clothing instead of warm

3. When the author says, "the old woman went at him like she did her garden" (lines 65–66), she most nearly means Mrs. Kohler:

   (F) determined to rid Professor Wunsch of his less desirable qualities.

   (G) tried in vain to improve his appearance.

   (H) spruced him up with care and attention.

   (J) tried to mold him into her idea of perfection.

4. Mrs. Kohler's garden is best described as a:

   (A) haven where she hid, planned, and found purpose.

   (B) reminder of her homeland, filled with hedges, fruit trees, and sage-brush.

   (C) barren sand gulch that she fled to when she was lonely.

   (D) verdant paradise fed by Moonstone's frequent rainfall.

5. The author would most likely say that Thea differed from other children in that she:

   (A) had few friends and attended few social gatherings.

   (B) studied music with Professor Wunsch.

   (C) was particularly fond of fairy tales.

   (D) was musically gifted.

Passage II — Social Science

Passage A

This passage is adapted from *Posttraumatic Stress Disorder: Issues and Controversies*, edited by Gerald M. Rosen (2004).

Controversy has haunted the diagnosis of post-traumatic stress disorder (PTSD) ever since its first appearance in the third edition of the *Diagnostic and Statistical Manual of Mental Disorders* (05) (*DSM-III*). At the outset, psychiatrists opposed to the inclusion of the diagnosis in the *DSM-III* argued that the problems of trauma-exposed people were already covered by combinations of existing diagnoses.

Ratifying PTSD would merely entail cobbling (10) together selected symptoms in people suffering from multiple disorders (for example, phobias, depression, and personality disorders) and then attributing these familiar problems to a traumatic event. Moreover, the very fact that the movement (15) to include the diagnosis in the *DSM-III* arose from Vietnam veterans' advocacy groups working with antiwar psychiatrists prompted concerns that PTSD was more of a political or social construct rather than a medical disease discovered in nature. (20)

Although the aforementioned two concerns have again resurfaced in contemporary debates about PTSD, additional issues have arisen as well. For example, the concept of a traumatic stressor has broadened to such an extent that, today, (25)

the vast majority of American adults have been exposed to PTSD-qualifying events. This state of affairs is drastically different from the late 1970s and early 1980s, when the concept of trauma was
(30) confined to catastrophic events falling outside the perimeter of everyday experience. Early 21st-century scholars are raising fresh questions about the syndromic validity of PTSD.

Passage B

This passage is adapted from *Post-Traumatic Stress Disorder*, edited by Dan J. Stein MD, PhD, Matthew J. Friedman, MD, and Carlos Blanco, MD, PhD (2011).

Of the many diagnoses in the *Diagnostic and*
(35) *Statistical Manual of Mental Disorders* (*DSM–III*), very few invoke an aetiology in their diagnostic criteria: (i) organic mental disorders (caused, for example, by a neurological abnormality); (ii) substance-use disorders (caused, for example, by psychoactive
(40) chemical agents); (iii) post-traumatic stress disorder (PTSD); (iv) acute stress disorder (ASD); and (v) adjustment disorders (ADs). The latter three are all caused by exposure to a stressful environmental event that exceeds the coping capacity of the
(45) affected individual. The presumed causal relationship between the stressor and PTSD, ASD, and AD is complicated and controversial. Controversy notwithstanding, acceptance of this causal relationship has equipped practitioners and scientists with
(50) a conceptual tool that has profoundly influenced clinical practice over the past 30 years.

PTSD is primarily a disorder of reactivity rather than of an altered baseline state, as in major depressive disorder or general anxiety disorder.
(55) Its psychopathology is characteristically expressed during interactions with the interpersonal or physical environment. People with PTSD are consumed by concerns about personal safety. They persistently scan the environment for threatening
(60) stimuli. When in doubt, they are more likely to assume that danger is present and will react accordingly. Avoidance and hyper-arousal symptoms can be understood within this context. The primacy of traumatic over other memories (for example, the
(65) re-experiencing symptoms) can also be understood as a pathological exaggeration of an adaptive human response to remember as much as possible about dangerous encounters in order to avoid similar threats in the future.

6. The author's attitude in Passage A can best be described as:

(F) contemplative.

(G) indecisive.

(H) explanatory.

(J) argumentative.

7. *Aetiology*, as it appears in the first sentence of Passage B, most likely means:

(F) that which creates controversy.

(G) the cause, manner, or set of causes that lead to a disease or condition.

(H) the study of the origin of words.

(J) an abnormality.

8. Which of the following best demonstrates the different perspectives between the psychiatrists and scholars mentioned in Passage A and the author of Passage B?

(A) The psychiatrists in Passage A think that the definition of PTSD has become too broad, while the author of Passage B feels it is a legitimate condition that has played an important role in clinical practice.

(B) The psychiatrists and scholars in Passage A believe that PTSD is a genuinely debilitating condition, while the author of Passage B believes today's doctors are too quick to offer up a PTSD diagnosis.

(C) The psychiatrists and scholars in Passage A believe that PTSD is simply a combination of other existing conditions, while the author of Passage B feels that PTSD is a disorder of an altered baseline state.

(D) The psychiatrists and scholars in Passage A believe that social conditions led to the theory behind PTSD, while the author of Passage B believes it was politics.

9. The authors of either Passage A or Passage B make all of the following assertions about the *Diagnostic and Statistical Manual of Mental Disorders* (*DSM–III*) EXCEPT:

(A) that few diagnoses listed also list causes.

(B) that psychiatrists initially did not want PTSD listed in the publication.

(C) that PTSD appeared in its third edition.

(D) that the information it contains about PTSD is wholly insufficient.

GO ON TO NEXT PAGE ➡

10. Which of the following statements is consistent with information contained in both passages?

    (F) PTSD is caused by stressful factors that exceed one's ability to cope, and scientists and medical professionals are often too quick to make the proper diagnosis.

    (G) PTSD is an increasingly prevalent problem in America, and years of research must be devoted to its causes and treatment.

    (H) The PTSD diagnosis is a controversial one, and scientists and medical professionals have differing opinions on its causes and its inclusion in the *Diagnostic and Statistical Manual of Mental Disorders* (*DSM-III*).

    (J) Scientists and medical professionals disagree over which stressors are sufficient to lead to PTSD.

Passage III — Humanities

Line   Adapting literature for the screen can be daunting. To increase one's chances of creating a successful adaptation, Linda Seger suggests choosing original works with a good story. In her book, (05) *The Art of Adaptation*, Seger goes on to clarify that a good story contains three elements: a goal, a problem or an issue, and a life-altering journey.

    Almost every aspect of life is touched by change. Outer physical change is readily apparent: (10) Babies grow into adults, winter becomes spring, natural structures build up and erode. Less tangible but not less important are the inner changes that human beings experience. Just as a disruption of normal physical growth is unhealthy, so is a lack of (15) inner growth. Although inner growth and change is healthy and exciting, it also requires courage and discernment. Journeying from a familiar state to a different one means sacrificing what is known and comfortable for something that is unknown and (20) uncertain, and this transformation involves risk. Inner growth comes at a price, and humans face a fundamental dilemma: To change requires a sacrifice of the old and familiar, but to remain static is to sacrifice a chance at new life.

(25)   Experiencing myth and ritual in film may assist people with this universal dilemma. According to Joseph Campbell in his book The Hero with a Thousand Faces, the purpose and effect of myth and ritual ". . . was to conduct people across those

difficult thresholds of transformation that demand (30) a change in the patterns not only of conscious but also of unconscious life." Myth serves to draw people into and through the important transformation journey.

    Through an examination of myths and rituals, (35) Campbell distinguishes what he called the monomyth, a heroic quest for an immensely precious treasure at high personal cost. The hero of the monomyth endures a series of trials and even death or a death-like experience that liberates the (40) hero from the past limitations of his old existence and renews life's possibilities. Mythology not only documents the transformation process of a mythic hero but also provides a means for other people to experience the hero's transformation. (45)

    Campbell claims it is "the prime function of mythology and rite to supply the symbols that carry the human spirit forward, in counteraction to those other constant human fantasies that tend to tie it back." Myth may carry out this function by (50) providing a vicarious heroic journey for the one who encounters myth in film adaptations of literary works. As viewers experience the transformations of film characters, they may gain insight into possibilities for their own heroic quests and, (55) through contact with the stories of others, may embark on their own transformational journeys into more mature human beings.

11. The author's primary purpose in writing this passage is most likely to:

    (A) establish that to create a well-executed screen adaptation, one should choose a story modeled on a mythological journey.

    (B) show that positive change is not possible without taking risks.

    (C) warn that screenwriters should not attempt to adapt literary works that do not contain a mythic journey.

    (D) reveal that a good film adaptation contains a series of trials and a near-death experience.

12. The author of the passage suggests that inner growth requires:

(F) an unhealthy forfeiture of established patterns of living and an acceptance of necessary risks.

(G) viewing film adaptations of literary works.

(H) courage to remain constant in changeable and unfamiliar environments.

(J) sacrifice of one's comfortable fantasies and the exploration of uncharted territory.

13. With which of the following statements would the author of the passage most likely agree?

(F) Mythology provides a way for others to benefit from the hero's metamorphosis.

(G) The three main elements of a good story are a life-altering journey, a serious problem, and a protagonist with whom the reader can empathize.

(H) Outer change is less significant but easier to achieve than inner change.

(J) Widely loved stories, if done well, produce remarkably successful screen adaptations.

14. According to Campbell, the purpose of ritual is to:

(F) transform a person's unintentional patterns.

(G) give people the tools to help others cross difficult thresholds in their lives.

(H) force people to break bad habits.

(J) promote a rich fantasy life.

15. Based on information in the passage, Linda Seger is most likely which of the following?

(F) Mythic hero

(G) Film script consultant

(H) Book critic

(J) Psychologist

Passage IV — Natural Science

This passage is adapted from *Reading the Weather*, by T. Morris Lonstreth.

Line

If there is anything that has been overlooked more than another it is our atmosphere. But it ab- solutely cannot be avoided, because if it were not for the atmosphere this earth of ours would be a wizened and sterile lump. (05)

To be sure the earth does not loom very large in the eye of the sun. It receives a positively trifling fraction of the total output of sunheat. So neg- ligible is this amount that it would not be worth our mentioning if we did not owe our existence to (10) it. It is thanks to the atmosphere, however, that the earth attains this (borrowed) importance. It is thanks to this thin layer of gases that we are protected from that fraction of sunheat which, however insignificant when compared with the (15) whole, would otherwise be sufficient to fry us all in a second. Without this gas wrapping, we would all freeze (if still unfried) immediately after sun- set. The atmosphere keeps us in a sort of thermos globe, unmindful of the burning power of the great (20) star, and of the uncalculated cold of outer space.

Yet, limitless as it seems to us, our invaluable atmosphere is a small thing after all. Half of its total bulk is compressed into the first three and a half miles upward. Only one sixty-fourth of it lies above (25) the twenty-one mile limit. Compared with the thick- ness of the earth this makes a very thin envelope.

Light as air, we say, forgetting that this stuff that looks so inconsequential weighs fifteen pounds to the square inch. The only reason that (30) we don't crumble is because the gases press evenly in all directions, thereby supporting this crush- ing burden. A layer of water thirty-four feet thick weighs just about as much as this air-pack under which we feel so buoyant. But if these gases get in (35) motion we feel their pressure.

As it blows along the surface of the earth this wind is mostly nitrogen, oxygen, moisture, and dust. The nitrogen occupies nearly eight-tenths of a given bulk of air, the oxygen two-tenths, and the (40) moisture anything up to one-twentieth. Five other gases are present in small quantities. The dust and the water vapor occupy space independently of the rest. As one goes up mountains the water vapor increases for a couple of thousand feet and then de- (45) creases to the seven mile limit after which it has al- most completely vanished. The lightest gases have been detected as high up as two hundred miles and scientists think that hydrogen, the lightest of all, may escape altogether from the restraint of gravity. (50)

At first glance the extreme readiness of the at- mosphere to carry dust and bacteria does not seem a point in its favor. In reality it is. Most bacteria

GO ON TO NEXT PAGE

are really allies of the human race. They benefit us
(55) by producing fermentations and disintegrations
of soils that prepare them for plant food. It is a
pity that the few disease breeding types of bacteria
should have given the family a bad name. Without
bacteria the sheltering atmosphere would have
(60) nothing but desert rock to protect.

Further, rain is accounted for only by the dust.
Of course this sounds very near the world's record
in absurdities. But it is a half-truth at least, for
moisture cannot condense on nothing. Every drop
(65) of rain, every globule of mist must have a nucleus.
Consequently each wind that blows, each volcano
that erupts is laying up dust for a rainy day. Ap-
parently the atmosphere is empty. Actually it is full
enough of dust-nuclei to outfit a full-grown fog
(70) if the dew point should be favorable. If there were
no dust in the air all shadows would be intensest
black, the sunlight blinding.

But the dust particles fulfill their greatest
mission as heat collectors — they and the particles
(75) of water vapor which have embraced them. It is
in reality owing to these water globules and not
to the atmosphere that supports them that we are
enabled to live in such comfortable temperatures.

So it comes about that the heavy moist air near
(80) the earth is the warmest of all. So high altitudes
and low temperatures are found together. But after
the limit of moisture content has been reached the
temperature gets no lower according to reliable
investigations. Instead a monotony of 459° below
(85) zero eternally prevails –459° is called the absolute
zero of space.

The vertical heating arrangements of the atmosphere appear somewhat irregular. But horizontally it is in a much worse way. The surface of
(90) the globe is three quarters water and one quarter
land and irregularly arranged at that. The shiny
water surfaces reflect a good deal of the heat which
they receive, they use up the heat in evaporation
and what they do absorb penetrates far. The land
(95) surfaces, on the contrary, absorb most of the heat
received, but it does not penetrate to any depth. As
a consequence of these differences, land warms up
about four times as quickly as water and cools off
about four times as fast. Therefore, the tempera-
(100) ture of air over continents is liable to much more
rapid and extreme changes than the air over the
oceans.

16. The primary purpose of the passage is to:

(A) explain why the earth's temperatures
rise and fall.

(B) highlight the role of dust particles in
determining the weather.

(C) explore the many roles of bacteria.

(D) describe the role of the earth's
atmosphere.

17. The author makes all of the following assertions about dust EXCEPT:

(F) dust plays a larger role in producing warm temperatures than the
atmosphere.

(G) dust accounts for only rain.

(H) particles of dust form the nucleus of rain
droplets.

(J) volcanic eruptions and blowing winds
are some of the sources of dust layers.

18. According to the passage, what does the author
consider dust's most important role?

(F) Serving as a heat collector.

(G) Forming the basis of rain.

(H) Minimizing the sun's glare.

(J) Providing a thick layer of protection
around the earth.

19. Which of the following does the author consider one of the world's absurdities?

(A) Without dust, sunlight would be
blinding.

(B) The irregularly configured surface of the
earth is made up of three quarters water
and one quarter land.

(C) Air temperatures over vast expanses of
land are prone to much more rapid and
extreme changes than the temperatures
over oceans.

(D) No other factors but dust account for the
presence of rain.

20. The word *trifling* in line 7 most likely means

(F) shallow.

(G) insignificant.

(H) silly.

(J) novel.

Science Test

Passage I

A conductivity meter measures the electrical conductivity in a solution and is used to measure the number of impurities in freshwater. One way to purify water is to remove ions. A solution with a higher ion content has a higher conductivity than a solution with fewer ions. A group of scientists studied water solution samples from 3 different sites from which they took 3 separate measurements — temperature in degrees Celsius, conductivity ($\mu S / m$), and species richness (number of invertebrate species found) — 10 different times. Site 1 was located 5 kilometers upstream of the city center, Site 2 was located in the city center, and Site 3 was 5 kilometers downstream of the city center.

Temperature and conductivity were measured with a conductivity meter. Species richness was collected, and invertebrates were placed in 98% ethanol to preserve the specimens. The collection was taken to the lab and dissecting microscopes were used to count and identify the invertebrate species. The results are shown in Table 1.

1. Based on Table 1, in Site 1, as the temperature of the solution increased, conductivity:

   (A) increased only.
   (B) decreased only.
   (C) stayed the same.
   (D) varied with no general trend.

TABLE 1

Site 1: Upstream			Site 2: City Center			Site 3: Downstream		
Temperature (Celsius)	Conductivity ($\mu S/m$)	Species Richness	Temperature (Celsius)	Conductivity ($\mu S/m$)	Species Richness	Temperature (Celsius)	Conductivity ($\mu S/m$)	Species Richness
23	200	10	25	900	1	22	655	5
23	155	12	24	800	2	23.5	599	4
24	220	11	23	821	1	22.5	621	6
23.5	185	9	23	906	3	25	632	4
24	188	10	24	855	2	25	588	5
22.5	190	11	22	899	1	24	612	7
25	203	14	23	865	4	23	641	6
24	253	12	24	845	1	23	625	5
23	211	10	22	933	2	23.5	598	4
25	177	8	23	865	2	24	600	3
23.7	198.2	10.7	23.3	868.9	1.9	23.6	617.1	4.9

GO ON TO NEXT PAGE

2. The scientists' research suggests that the collection site or sites whose water solution contains the greatest number of impurities is/are:

(F) Site 1

(G) Site 2

(H) Site 3

(J) Site 1 and Site 3

3. The conductivity of typical drinking water ranges between 50 and 500 $\mu S / m$. Based on the results of the scientists' research, which of the three sites contain(s) water solutions that may be safe to drink?

(A) Site 1 only

(B) Site 3 only

(C) Site 1 and Site 2

(D) Site 2 and Site 3

4. Suppose an additional study was conducted in the same manner at a site located in rural pastureland several miles upstream from Site 1. The average conductivity of this site was measured to be 500 $\mu S / m$. The average species richness of this new site would most likely be:

(F) less than 1.9.

(G) between 1.9 and 4.9.

(H) between 4.9 and 10.7.

(J) greater than 10.7.

5. Based on the results of the research, which abiotic factor generally correlated to species richness?

(A) Only temperature correlated to species richness.

(B) Only conductivity correlated to species richness.

(C) Both temperature and conductivity correlated to species richness.

(D) No abiotic factors correlated to species richness.

6. The scientists most likely used which of the following to collect the data necessary to determine species richness?

(F) Balance

(G) pH meter

(H) Nets

(J) Thermometer

Passage II

Convict cichlids are highly aggressive freshwater fish that are found in streams and rivers in Central America. Their aggression allows them to protect their breeding territory from intruders that enter and consume their offspring. Both males and females are aggressive, and aggressiveness is also related to size.

Experiment 1

Researchers collected 30 males and 30 females and separated them into 3 categories based on size: small (50–69 mm), medium (70–89 mm), and large (90–109 mm). They allowed one fish (the focal fish) to claim a territory in an aquarium tank for 5 days. On day 6, they placed an intruder of equal size to and of the same sex as the focal fish into the aquarium and watched the aggressive behaviors for 30 minutes. Aggressive behaviors viewed were lateral displays, frontal displays, biting, mouth wrestling, and chasing. All behaviors were lumped together and the total time spent in these behaviors was averaged for each group. Table 1 records the findings of average number of minutes within 30-minute time periods that the convict cichlid fish exhibited acts of aggression based on size and sex.

TABLE 1

	Small (50–69 mm) Focal Fish & Intruder	Medium (70–89 mm) Focal Fish & Intruder	Large (90–109 mm) Focal Fish & Intruder
Males	12	18	23
Females	6	10	14

Experiment 2

Researchers repeated Experiment 1 but varied the size of the intruder they introduced into the tank on day 6. In the study, 10 females and 10 males received an intruder that was 20 mm smaller than the focal fish, 10 females and 10 males received an equal-sized intruder, and 10 males and 10 females received an intruder that was 20 mm larger than the focal fish. All intruders were the same sex as the focal fish. The same types of aggressive behaviors as those in Experiment 1 were observed for 30 minutes and recorded. Behaviors were grouped together, and the total time spent in these behaviors was averaged for each group. Table 2 records average number of minutes of aggression within a 30-minute time period in convict cichlid fish based on intruder size and sex.

TABLE 2

	Intruder 20 mm Smaller than Focal Fish	Equal-Sized Intruder	Intruder 20 mm Larger than Focal Fish
Males	12	20	11
Females	6	11	5

7. The two experiments were likely designed to answer which of these questions?

(A) Are highly aggressive fish more likely to exist in fresh or saltwater?

(B) What are the most common types of aggressive behaviors exhibited by convict cichlids?

(C) Is size or gender a better indicator of the potential for aggression in convict cichlids?

(D) How does the relative size of an intruder fish affect the number of aggressive behaviors exhibited by a focal fish?

8. According to Experiment 1, which of the following is the correct order of cichlids from highest to lowest aggression?

(F) Large female, large male, medium female, small male.

(G) Large male, large female, medium male, small female.

(H) Large male, medium male, large female, small male.

(J) Large male, medium male, small male, large female.

9. Based on Experiment 1 and Experiment 2, male cichlids exhibited:

(A) about half as much aggression as female cichlids.

(B) about twice as much aggression as female cichlids.

(C) about the same amount of aggression as female cichlids.

(D) about half as much aggression as female cichlids in Experiment 2 and about twice as much aggression as female cichlids in Experiment 1.

10. Experiment 1 and Experiment 2 differed in that Experiment 2 varied which independent variable?

(F) Gender of the intruder.

(G) Relative size of the intruder to focal fish.

(H) Level of aggression in the intruder.

(J) Number of days provided for the focal fish to establish its territory.

11. In Experiment 2, the recorded amount of aggression was influenced primarily by:

(A) the gender and size of the focal fish.

(B) only the gender of the focal fish.

(C) only the size of the intruder.

(D) the gender of the focal fish and the size of the intruder.

GO ON TO NEXT PAGE

12. The scientists who conducted the research wanted to use the lab data to determine which combination of two cichlids would be the best protectors of their offspring. Based on the results of the two experiments, which of the following pairs was the one the scientists likely concluded was the best?

(F) Medium male paired with a large female.

(G) Large male paired with a small female.

(H) Medium male paired with a medium female.

(J) Small male paired with a small female.

13. Where solid bars represent male cichlids and patterned bars represent female cichlids, which of the following graphs provides the most accurate representation of the results of Experiment 2?

(A)
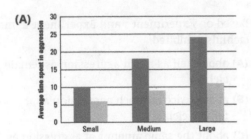

(B)
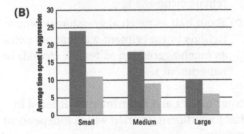

(C)
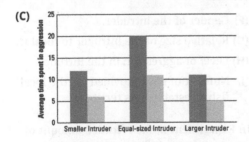

(D)
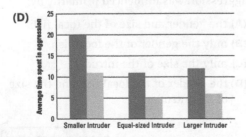

Passage III

Genetically modified organisms (GMOs) are any organisms that are modified with respect to their genetics. A wide range of methods exist for producing GMOs, from procedures as simple as selective breeding (which has been conducted for thousands of years) to the more recent technology of inserting genes of one organism into those of another organism. GMOs have been used to produce medical advances such as creating insulin for people with diabetes. However, more recently there have been debates over the role GMOs should play in foods.

Two researchers present their opinions.

Researcher 1

GMO foods were first designed in an attempt to control pests without using pesticides. Traditional pesticides can be harmful to the environment, so reducing pesticides would provide significant environmental benefits. In addition, GMO foods are thought to increase crop yields. Given that our world population continues to grow exponentially, food may become a limited resource and using genetically modified foods may assist in the sustenance of an exploding global population. GMOs have been a part of food production for several decades, and no scientific evidence exists to support the view that the nutritional value of GMOs is less than that of food that has not been genetically modified. Nor does evidence suggest that GMOs cause harm to the organisms that consume them. Some studies have reported minor increases in food allergies associated with GMOs, but that information is likely correlational, not causational.

Researcher 2

Genetically modified foods may have been first implemented to replace pesticides, but recent data shows that pests become resistant to the GMO plants more quickly than to plants that have not been genetically modified and are treated with pesticides. Reducing pesticides benefits the environment, but this reduction can be achieved without resorting to producing GMOs. Planting a variety of species instead of monocultures and using natural pest repellants (e.g., lady bugs) would reduce pesticide use in a better way than GMOs. Not all GMOs yield higher crops, and other options to combat limited food production, such as home and community gardening, exist. Placing the burden of food production on individuals would reduce the strain on big corporations. Recent efforts in urban areas include converting spaces on rooftops to community farms. Although current studies show no direct correlation between GMOs and health problems in humans, GMOs have not been studied long enough to rule out the possibility of long-term effects. The nutritional value of GMOs may be similar to that of organically grown food, but the taste and overall quality are not. Anyone who has eaten both organic foods and GMOs will attest to the former's superiority. The last problem with GMOs is that cross contamination can occur. Plant pollen can travel long distances and GMO plants can hybridize with organic crops.

14. According to Researcher 1, what are the benefits of GMOs?

(F) They reduce pesticide use and increase crop yields.

(G) They increase pesticide use and decrease crop yields.

(H) They increase the nutritional value of food and do not cause harm to organisms.

(J) Researcher 1 sees no benefits of GMOs.

15. According to the passage, with which of the following statements would both researchers agree?

(A) Increasing pesticide use would be good for the environment.

(B) There is no direct correlation between GMOs and health problems in humans.

(C) GMO foods have improved taste and quality.

(D) GMO foods increase food allergies in many of the humans who consume them.

16. According to Researcher 2, a major disadvantage of GMOs is that:

(F) their pollen can travel long distances.

(G) their use decreases the number of naturally occurring pest reducers.

(H) their use increases the prevalence of harmful pesticides.

(J) they are directly correlated with health problems in humans.

17. According to Researcher 1, a harmful effect that may be correlated to GMO foods is:

(A) pesticide resistance.

(B) production of tumors in consumers.

(C) decreased nutritional value.

(D) increased food allergies in consumers.

18. According to Researcher 2, the use of pesticides may be reduced by all of the following EXCEPT:

(F) replacing only some organically grown crops with GMOs.

(G) planting a variety of species instead of monocultures.

(H) using ladybugs as repellants.

(J) increasing the number of community farms.

19. According to Researcher 2, GMOs have been linked to which of the following?

(A) An increase in the number of pesticides.

(B) An increase in the number of home and community gardens.

(C) Inferior food quality.

(D) A larger burden placed on food-producing corporations.

GO ON TO NEXT PAGE

20. Which of the following graphs is consistent with Researcher 1's view but not Researcher 2's?

(A)

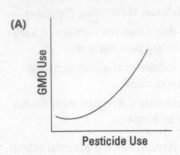

(B)

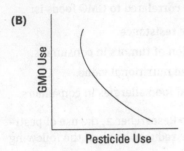

(C)

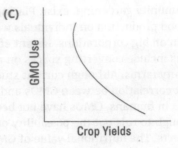

(D)

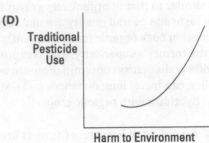

Writing Test

TIME: 40 minutes

DIRECTIONS: Respond to the following prompt with a well-organized essay that follows the rules of Standard English. Write your essay on a separate sheet of lined paper.

Some people believe that the elderly population should be required to reapply for a driver's license and retake a driving test after they reach a particular age. As the Baby Boomer generation ages, more and more elderly drivers are taking to the roadways, and with the aging process comes a variety of issues that can lead to problems behind the wheel. Hearing loss, diminished vision, and longer reaction times are just a few of these possible concerns. Is it fair to force an entire population to reapply for something they have already earned and been using for decades? Given the increasing number of elderly drivers on the road, this is an important issue worthy of careful consideration.

Read and carefully consider these perspectives. Each suggests a particular way of thinking about whether elderly drivers should have to reapply for a driver's license once they reach a certain age.

Perspective 1: Elderly drivers should have to retake their driving tests once they reach a particular age for both their own safety and that of all others out on the roadways. Certain abilities decrease with age, and many of those abilities that do decrease are critical for maintaining safe driving practices.

Perspective 2: Forcing elderly drivers to retake their driving tests based on age, rather than a demonstrated lack of ability behind the wheel, is essentially a form of age discrimination and should not be put into practice.

Perspective 3: Requiring all elderly drivers to reapply for driver's licenses after they reach a given age puts an unnecessary strain on already limited resources in our DMVs and driving schools, and it would take attention away from the inexperienced teen population that is learning the rules of the road for the first time.

Essay Task

Write a unified, coherent essay in which you evaluate multiple perspectives as to whether elderly drivers should be forced to reapply for a driver's license once they reach a given age. In your essay, be sure to:

- Clearly state your own perspective on the issue and analyze the relationship between your perspective and at least one other perspective.

- Develop and support your ideas with reasoning and examples.

- Organize your ideas clearly and logically.

- Communicate your ideas effectively in standard written English.

Your perspective may be in full agreement with any of the others, in partial agreement, or wholly different.

Answers and Explanations

In this section, we provide detailed answer explanations for each problem on the shortened practice test to help you understand why one answer is correct and the others aren't. Along the way, you find zillions of tips, traps, and other valuable information you can use when you face the actual exam on test day. So be sure to read all the explanations carefully — yes, even the ones you got right!

English Test

1. **B.** The underlined part contains a semicolon, so you're likely dealing with proper punctuation. For the semicolon to be proper, the words before it and after it must express a complete thought. The words after the semicolon make up an independent clause; they have a subject *methods* and a verb *are* and don't begin with a subordinating conjunction. But the words before the semicolon begin with the subordinating conjunction *when*, so even though they have the subject and verb *it comes*, they don't form a complete thought. The semicolon is wrong and so are the colon and dash. The proper way to separate a beginning dependent clause from the rest of the sentence is with a comma. Choice (B) is correct. To review punctuation rules, flip to Block 2.

2. **H.** When you see *being* in an answer choice, that answer is almost always wrong. *Being* by itself doesn't function as a verb, so the sentence as provided has no verb. The same problem applies to Choice (J). The only option that gives the sentence a verb is Choice (H).

   REMEMBER

   When *ing* verbs such as *being* appear in sentences without the assistance of those trusty helping verbs, they can't function as verbs and complete the sentence. Always check sentences with *ing* verbs to make sure they include a helping verb to carry the load.

3. **A.** Quickly eliminate Choice (C). The form *its'* doesn't exist. Then check the pronoun *it* in the underlined portion. You know the contraction form (*it's*) is okay because you substitute *it is* for *it's* and the sentence sounds just fine. Eliminate Choice (B) because it contains the possessive form of *it*. Choice (D) has the proper form of *it*, but it improperly separates the beginning dependent clause from the rest of the sentence with a semicolon instead of a comma. Choice (A) is best.

4. **H.** The underlined word is ambiguous — *one* what? The pronouns offered by Choices (G) and (J) don't provide clarity, so the best answer is the clearly-stated noun in Choice (H).

5. **A.** The predominate question you ask yourself for an addition question is whether the proposed addition's topic is relevant to the substance of the paragraph. The paragraph is about finding a personal trainer, and the new sentence relates to that topic. So you can eliminate Choices (C) and (D). Of the two remaining answers, Choice (A) is best because the sentence offers ways to find a personal trainer rather than the benefits of using one.

6. **G.** When you encounter questions that ask for the least appropriate answer, find the option that has a different meaning from the other ones. The original word is *capable*, which means skilled or experienced. *Competent* is also a synonym. So eliminate those answers. The option that has a slightly different meaning is *useful*. To be of use isn't the same as being able. Choice (G) doesn't fit.

7. **B.** To communicate well and communicate clearly mean roughly the same thing, so Choice (A) is redundant. Choice (C) is redundant and improper because it uses the adjective *clear* to describe the verb *communicate*. Both Choices (B) and (D) eliminate the redundancy, but Choice (B) does so more precisely (think fewest words).

8. **G.** An underlined verb usually signals you to check for subject/verb agreement and verb tense issues. The verbs agree in number with *you*, so look for the proper tense. The rest of the paragraph is in present tense, which means the verb in this sentence should be too. Choice (G) is correct.

9. **D.** The underlined part is a transition. To pick the best transition, check the sentence or sentences before it and the sentence that contains it. The answer that brings the two thoughts together best is the correct transition. The idea before the transition is that you may wish to choose a trainer with a similar physique. Staying on track isn't an example of choosing someone with a similar body shape, so Choice (A) doesn't work. Choice (C) provides the same transition, so it must be wrong. Choice (B) shows contrast, and the ideas aren't opposite. The best solution is to eliminate the transition altogether.

TIP

If the answer choices contain two similar transition words, eliminate both. You can't have two right answers, so they must both be wrong.

10. **F.** To determine the best transition sentence, focus first on the paragraph it introduces. The following sentences provide information about the different personalities and styles of trainers. It's not about credentials, facilities, or missing workouts, so the best answer is Choice (F).

11. **C.** The underlined part creates a comma splice. The words before and after the comma both express complete thoughts. So Choice (A) is out. Choice (B) doesn't correct the punctuation problem. Rule out Choice (D) because a comma after an *and* that joins two complete thoughts is rarely proper. The answer has to be Choice (C). It fixes the comma splice by inserting a conjunction between the two independent clauses and doesn't create another punctuation error.

12. **H.** Choice (J) is irrelevant; nothing in the essay discusses healthy or unhealthy eating habits. Choice (F) deals with only one aspect of the preceding paragraphs, so it's not the best conclusion for the whole paragraph. Between Choices (G) and (H), Choice (H) is better. It more clearly sets up the topic of the next paragraph: deciding whether a trainer is a good fit.

13. **B.** The answer choices are the same but for the commas. The underlined part is a beginning prepositional phrase, so it should be separated from the rest of the sentence with a comma at the end. Choice (C) is out because it doesn't have a comma at the end of the phrase. Choice (D) sticks a comma between a subject *trainer* and its *verb will be*, so it can't be right. The comma between *decide* and *whether* in Choice (A) serves no purpose. The best answer is Choice (B); it places the comma at the end of the phrase and contains no unnecessary additional punctuation.

14. **J.** When you see an underlined verb, first check for subject/verb agreement. The subject of the sentence is compound: *weight loss and physical fitness*. Compound subjects take plural verbs. Don't be fooled by the ending *s*; the verb *starts* is singular. *Begins* is also singular. Choices (F) and (G) are wrong. Choice (H) tries to replace the verb with an *ing* word that can't work as a verb on its own. The answer is the plural verb *start* in Choice (J).

15. **D.** This big picture question actually asks you about the passage's main purpose. Focus on the exact language of the question and ask yourself whether the essay highlights some of the best ways to lose weight. It talks about one way to lose weight, but it doesn't go into any others. The correct answer likely begins with *No*. When you check Choices (C) and (D), you see that Choice (D) is the better answer. The essay only highlights one weight loss method, so it wouldn't provide much information about more than one way to lose weight.

16. G. In the underlined part, you have two nouns smack dab next to each other. Whenever you see a noun following another noun, the first noun is almost always possessive. Choice (G) puts the first noun in possessive form, so it's the right answer. Choice (H) uses the possessive form improperly.

A noun that's the object of a preposition (in this case *of*) is never possessive.

REMEMBER

17. C. The placement of a comma before a coordinating conjunction such as *and*, *but*, or *or* is only proper when the conjunction joins two complete thoughts. *Known as America's pastime* isn't a complete thought, so beginning the underlined part with a conjunction can't be right. Eliminate Choices (A) and (B). If you omit the underlined words, the subject of the sentence becomes *known* and *means* is the verb. If that isn't bad enough, Choice (D) also separates the subject and verb with a single comma, which is never proper. Choice (C) is the answer that preserves *it* as the subject and doesn't commit any messy comma infractions.

18. G. Choices (F) and (J) contain punctuation problems, so you can eliminate them. Choice (F) is a run-on, and Choice (J) creates a comma splice. Punctuation is okay in Choices (G) and (H), so choose the better answer based on the transition it provides between the two thoughts. The cause-and-effect transition created by *therefore* makes more sense than the contrast suggested by *but*. So Choice (G) is correct.

19. A. Check the underlined possessive pronoun for proper form. *Their* renames *players*, so the plural format is proper and Choice (D) can't be right. The next step is to decide whether you need the possessive form. Because *skills* is a noun, the possessive form is necessary.

Whenever a noun immediately follows a pronoun or other noun, the first noun should be in possessive form.

REMEMBER

20. J. All of the choices are synonyms for *simulates*, but Choice (J) doesn't fit as well as the others. The definition of *fake* implies that the pitches would be false, which isn't exactly the same as the similarity suggested by the original sentence and the other three answers.

21. B. The underlined word is a verb. Subject/verb agreement isn't an issue, so check tense. The rest of the paragraph is in present tense. Choice (B) is also in present tense, so it's the best answer.

22. F. Choices (G), (H), and (J) add unnecessary words to the original construction. *While* suggests *at the same time*, so any words or phrases that restate the simultaneous actions are redundant. Stick with the original in Choice (A).

23. A. Determine whether the addition relates to the topic of the paragraph. The paragraph is about what to consider when selecting a machine, so the phrase is relevant. The answer is likely *yes*. When you double-check the *no* options, you see that neither is true. The addition isn't distracting nor is it repetitive. So check out the *yes* options. Choice (B) is out because the passage suggests that a pitching machine is beneficial for players of *all* ages. The addition clarifies the reasons to consider the age of the player, so you can feel confident in selecting Choice (A).

24. H. Eliminate Choice (J) immediately because "more slower" creates two comparative forms, adding *more* and *er* to the adjective. The comparative form of one-syllable words is usually to add *er* to the end rather than *more* to the end, so Choice (G) is out. Choices (G), (J), and (F) are all wrong, too, because they use an adjective to describe the verb *releases*. The only answer that properly provides an adverb to describe the verb is Choice (H).

Adjectives never define active verbs. Only adverbs do.

REMEMBER

25. **D.** *Advanced* and *elevated* have the same meaning, so it's redundant to use both. Eliminate Choices (A), (B), and (C) because they're repetitive and awkward. The solution is to eliminate the clause as suggested by Choice (D).

26. **J.** The lengthy underlined part appears in a sentence with a beginning participle (verb part) phrase. A beginning participle phrase *always* describes the subject of the sentence, so check the subject to see whether it makes sense that it would feature many customizable options. A *hitter*, *adjustments*, and *time* don't feature customizable options. Only *machines* can have customizable options. So Choice (J) is the only logical answer.

Whenever you see a lengthy underlined portion in a sentence with a participle phrase at the beginning, check for *dangling particles* — a phrase that doesn't logically describe the subject of the sentence.

27. **C.** Remember that you're looking for the answer that *doesn't* work. The proper preposition that fits with "to take part" is *in* not *of*. Therefore, the unacceptable answer is Choice (C).

The ACT often asks you to consider the proper use of prepositions, so when you see answer choices with different preposition options, determine which preposition fits the sentence.

28. **F.** If you can't quickly determine whether the proposed addition is relevant, check what comes after *because* in each answer to eliminate choices that aren't true. Choice (H) is a definite *no* because nowhere in the essay does the author stress that young players are more likely to benefit from pitching machines than older ones are. Eliminate Choice (G) because the author never claims that older players are more likely to experience the benefits of a pitching machine. Similarly, Choice (J) isn't true; the fourth paragraph doesn't contain a point that the suggested addition would build upon. Choice (F) is the best answer. The addition would contradict the author's statement in Paragraph 1 that pitching machines are a great resource for players at all levels.

29. **C.** Here's another redundancy error. In Choice (A), "want to" and "interest in" don't provide different information. *Interest* and *desire* have essentially the same meaning in Choice (B). To *aspire* and *endeavor* are similar verbs, so Choice (D) is also redundant. The only answer that isn't repetitive is Choice (C).

30. **F.** Notice *these* in the fifth paragraph. To properly reference "these pitching machines," the paragraph must follow another paragraph that introduces the machines. So Choice (G) must be wrong. The last paragraph sums up the points made elsewhere in the essay. A summary of points is usually included in the introduction or conclusion. You've already established that the paragraph can't be first, so it's best where it is now at the end of the passage.

Placing checkmarks in the essay for each of the possible positions for Paragraph 5 will save time. You won't have to continually check your answers for the potential options.

31. **C.** The underlined verb doesn't have a subject/verb agreement problem, so check the tense. The verb is in present perfect tense, which would indicate that Roosevelt's rising may still continue. Later you see that Roosevelt was around in 1900, so it's unlikely that he's still living, let alone rising. The correct tense is the simple past *rose*, Choice (C). Choice (D) is clearly incorrect because *has rose* isn't a proper verb construction, and Choice (B) can't be right because the other past actions in the paragraph are expressed in past tense.

32. **F.** To answer this question correctly, you need to know the meaning of *prominence*. *Prominence* is defined as "the state of being important or famous." While *infamy*, Choice (B), does mean "widely known," its connotation is negative, which doesn't match the tone of the passage or the author's overall impression of Teddy Roosevelt. Choices (C) and (D) are both antonyms of *prominence*, indicating that Teddy Roosevelt was not, in fact, very well known at all. The passage implies that Roosevelt was very well known, so stick with Choice (F) and leave the underlined portion as is.

33. **B.** Note that a comma exists before the underlined part, which means that *unit* is followed by a nonessential descriptive phrase. The element that describes *unit* is "the 'Rough Riders.'" So choose the answer that puts commas on both sides of that noun phrase. Choices (B) and (D) complete the task, but Choice (D) adds an incorrect comma after *Hill*. Choice (B) is best.

34. **H.** Inserting information about how and why McKinley was assassinated may be relevant to a passage about McKinley, but the passage is about Roosevelt and McKinley is not mentioned again. And how Roosevelt came to assume the presidency is not nearly as important as what he did once he had the job, so the proposed addition is irrelevant and Choices (F) and (G) are out. The passage doesn't mention McKinley elsewhere, so Choice (J) is wrong. Choice (H) is correct.

35. **D.** The proper way to construct the superlative form of a one-syllable word such as *young* is to add *–est* to the end. So the best answer is Choice (D).

36. **F.** The answer that is least like *exude* is Choice (F). All of the other choices mean something akin to "give off," but the meaning of *infuse* is slightly different. To infuse is to fill or "put in."

37. **C.** Don't let Choices (B) and (D) fool you. This question doesn't present a tense issue. The problem is parallelism. Each element of Roosevelt's description should be the same part of speech, and because *intelligent* and *well read* are adjectives, the correct answer must also be an adjective. Choice (C) provides parallel construction.

38. **J.** Note that the underlined part is an element of a series of activities Roosevelt participated in. To keep the series parallel, pick the activity expressed in Choice (J). Were you tempted by Choice (H)? Continuing the series with *engaging* seems to fit with the *–ing* construction of *participating*, but the third element doesn't begin with a gerund, so Choice (H) can't be correct.

REMEMBER

Every element of a series should begin with the same grammatical format to maximize parallel structure.

39. **B.** Did you notice that *active* and *busy* have essentially the same meaning? Including both adjectives doesn't enhance the sentence, so the best answer is the more succinct Choice (B).

TIP

An omit option in the answer choices usually signals redundancy. Be careful, though. Indeed this question involves redundancy, but omitting the underlined words doesn't take care of the problem and changes the intended meaning of the sentence. The sentence isn't about Roosevelt becoming one of the presidents in the history of the United States; its point is that he was one of the busiest. If you choose to omit, reread the sentence without the underlined part to make sure it makes sense.

40. **F.** The original is correct. Choice (G) introduces passive voice "topics that were tackled" instead of the active "topics he tackled." Choice (H) creates a problem with subject/verb agreement. The plural *topics* needs the plural verb *were*. Choice (J) uses far too many words to convey the same idea as Choice (F). The best answer is Choice (F).

41. B. The underlined part provides a transition, so read the sentence before it and the sentence it's a part of to see how the ideas in each sentence relate. The preceding sentence states that Roosevelt invited union members and mine owners to work out a solution. The next sentence states that the owners refused to speak with the union. The two ideas suggest contrast: Roosevelt invited them, *but* the owners refused. The best answer is *however* in Choice (B). For Choice (C) to be correct, the idea that the owners refused would have to be the final step in a series, but the events continue after the sentence with the underlined words. Choices (A) and (C) create a cause-and-effect relationship, but Roosevelt's invitation didn't cause the owners to refuse. Choice (B) is best.

TIP

Questions about transition words often contain two answers that provide the same transition. Once you determine that two answers are similar, you can eliminate both. Because they can't both be right, they must both be wrong.

42. F. Consider the message in the proposed deletion. The sentence concludes a detailed example of one of Roosevelt's accomplishments. Choice (F) states this purpose clearly. Choice (J) is wrong because the sentence contains specific information rather than general observations. Choice (H) is also incorrect. The next paragraph is about railroads rather than mines, so you know that the sentence doesn't foreshadow a subsequent point. Without the last sentence, the reader wouldn't know the outcome of the incident, so Choice (G) can't be correct.

TIP

The correct answer to a deletion question is rarely that the deleted material is irrelevant or unnecessary. If you choose such an answer, make sure the deleted portion has nothing to do with the topic of the paragraph.

43. B. The underlined word and answer choices are prepositions. Choose the one that fits the meaning of the sentence. Notice that the main verb *controlled* is in simple past tense. So the event happened at one point in time. Later in the paragraph, you discover that the law designed to deal with railroad control was finalized in 1906. The railroads couldn't have controlled prices after the beginning of the 20th century, so Choice (C) is wrong. Choices (A) and (D) suggest continuation over a long period rather than a specific point in time, so they don't work. The best answer is Choice (B), which properly conveys that the control existed specifically in the first years of the 20th century.

44. J. The underlined part provides a transition between the statement that Roosevelt believed that the system gave companies too much power and hurt consumers with the information that he supported an act that regulated the railroad. Eliminate Choices (G) and (H) because they provide the same transition. They can't both be right. The remaining choices suggest an example or a cause and effect. Supporting the act isn't an example of Roosevelt's belief. Instead, his belief is the *reason* for his support of the act. The best answer is Choice (J) because this shows cause and effect.

45. C. The apostrophes in the answer choices should clue you into checking for possessive form. The underlined word is a noun followed by the noun phrase "financial records." A noun followed by another noun or noun phrase almost always indicates possessive form. So your answer will contain an apostrophe and you can eliminate Choice (B). Choice (D) is wrong because the plural of *company* is *companies*. The remaining choices require you to determine whether the noun is plural or singular. It must be plural because if it were singular, it would be preceded by an article such as *the* or *a*. The way to make *companies* possessive is to end the word with an apostrophe. Choice (C) is correct.

TIP

When you see possessive form in the ACT English test answers, the correct answer will almost always be possessive. If you pick an answer that isn't possessive, double-check to make you haven't missed something.

Mathematics Test

1. **B.** According to the order of operations, exponential parts of the equation always must be solved before multiplication parts of the equation. Because $x = 3$, $2^x = 8$ because $2 \times 2 \times 2 = 8$. Next, that value must be multiplied by the value of y, which is 2, giving you the final answer of 16, which is Choice (B).

   Beware of Choice (E), which mixes up the order of operations by multiplying 2 and y and then raising the resulting value of 4 to the power of x.

2. **F.** A geometric series is a series of numbers in which each number is multiplied by a common value to determine the number that comes after it. In this particular geometric series, the first number is multiplied by 2 to find the second number, which is then multiplied by 2 to find the third number, and so on, because $0.75 \times 2 = 1.5$ and $1.5 \times 2 = 3$. Find the 5th term, then, by multiplying the 4th term (6) by 2 to get Choice (F), 12.

3. **A.** To find the measure of $\angle ABD$, you can set up an equation calling the measure of $\angle ABD = 3x$ and $\angle DBC = x$. $\angle ABD$ and $\angle DBC$ combine to measure 180° because A, B, and C are collinear. In this case, $3x + x = 180$. Simplify this equation to $4x = 180$. When you divide both sides by 4, you get $x = 45$. Don't stop there and pick Choice (E), though. That's the measure of $\angle DBC$. Multiply 45 by 3 to get 135°, which is the measure of $\angle ABD$.

   If you picked Choice (C), you incorrectly presumed that A, B, and C form a right angle.

4. **K.** Divide by multiplying 3 by $\frac{8}{3}$. The 3s cancel, so the answer is 8.

   Don't get caught picking Choice (J), which simplifies the 3 in the numerator and the 3 in the numerator of the denominator to equal 1. That's not the way to divide a fraction.

REMEMBER

   When you divide by a fraction, you solve by simply multiplying by the reciprocal of the second fraction.

5. **D.** Angle a and the 37° are supplementary, which means their sum measures 180°. So the measure of angle a is $180 - 37$ or 143°. Because lines C and D are parallel and crossed by a transversal, angle a corresponds with angle b, which means they have the same degree measure. So angle b also measures 143°.

6. **F.** Before you find the chance that Ross will pick 2 black socks, you first have to find the chance that the first sock he picks will be black. That chance is $\frac{2}{4}$ or $\frac{1}{2}$ because 2 out of 4 socks are black. Then, you have to multiply that fraction by the probability that the second sock will be black. Be careful, because the second probability isn't also $\frac{1}{2}$ because Ross has already picked a black sock from the drawer. After the first sock, only 3 socks remain in the drawer and only 1 is black. So the chance that the second sock he picks will be black is actually $\frac{1}{3}$. The chance that both socks Ross picks will be black can then be found by multiplying $\frac{1}{2}$ by $\frac{1}{3}$, which is $\frac{1}{6}$. Pick Choice (F).

7. D. This question concerns a simple right triangle. The following figure shows the values of the leg lengths.

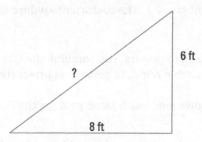

The ramp length is the hypotenuse. Memorize the 3-4-5 Pythagorean triple; ACT math questions incorporate it frequently. The lengths of the sides of this triangle are just those of the traditional 3-4-5 triangle times 2, so the missing side is 10 feet.

REMEMBER

If you don't remember Pythagorean triples, you can find the length of the ramp, which is the hypotenuse in this case, by plugging values into the Pythagorean theorem ($a^2 + b^2 = c^2$) and solving for c, but it's much faster to rely on common side ratios of right triangles.

8. J. To solve this expression, change the fractions so they have the same denominator. The least common denominator of this specific set of fractions is 6 because all three denominators evenly go into it. The first fraction doesn't change because its denominator is already 6, but $\frac{1}{2}$ converts to $\frac{3}{6}$ and $\frac{1}{3}$ converts to $\frac{2}{6}$. Your next task is to find the sum of $\frac{1}{6} + \frac{3}{6} + \frac{2}{6}$. When adding fractions with common denominators, just add the numerators and put the

sum over the common denominator. In this case, the answer is $\frac{6}{6}$, which simplifies to 1, Choice (J).

9. C. Rather than attempting to factor this complex quadratic, you can work more quickly by applying FOIL to all the answer possibilities. Start with the middle answer. You just need to figure out the middle term because the first and last terms of each answer choice are the same. The product of the outer terms of Choice (C) is $-6x$; the inner terms multiply to $2x$. The sum of the outer and inner terms is $-4x$, so Choice (C) is correct.

TIP

An alternative and possibly quicker way to factor quadratic equations when the coefficient of the first term is not 1 is called the "dream method." The dream method requires you to multiply the coefficient of the x^2 term by the last term in the quadratic. In this case, you multiply 4 by -3 to get -12. Then, set up blank terms that begin with the original coefficient of the original first term multiplied by the variable, like this: $(4x +)(4x +)$. Then find the factors of -12 that add up to the coefficient of the middle term in the original expression, in this case -4. These factors are 2 and -6. Place these values in the blank terms you just created to make $(4x + 2)(4x - 6)$. Then reduce each term as much as you can to get your final answer of $(2x + 1)(2x - 3)$.

10. J. Make answering this question quick and simple by noticing first that the point on the x-axis that also lies on the y-axis has an x-coordinate of 0. The x-coordinate is the first number in the ordered pair. Eliminate Choices (F), (G), and (K) because they don't have x-coordinates of 0. You know the answer is either Choice (H) or (J). Substitute 0 for x in the equation and solve for y. That gives you $0 + 4y = 28$ so $y = 7$. The point that $7x + 4y = 28$ intersects the y-axis is (0, 7), Choice (J).

You can also approach this problem by solving the original equation for y to put it in the format of the equation of a line: $y = mx + b$, where b is the y-intercept. When you solve for y, you get $y = -\frac{7}{4}x + 7$. So you know the y-intercept is 7. The only answer with a y-coordinate of 7 is Choice (C).

11. A. When simplifying expressions that involve only multiplication, you can simply combine like variables. First, multiply the numerators to get $3x^4y^2$. Then multiply the denominators to get $6y$. Divide the y terms: $\frac{y^2}{y} = y$. The coefficients reduce to $\frac{1}{2}$ to make the final answer $\frac{x^4y}{2}$.

REMEMBER

When you multiply the same variable raised to powers, you combine the terms by simply adding the powers. To divide the same variable raised to powers, subtract the exponents.

12. C. The correct formula is the one that shows how much Jacob paid for the flour, sugar, and trays.

If the proper formula isn't immediately obvious to you, you could spend a whole bunch of time trying to figure it out. Or you could save some time and substitute numbers for the variables in the problem to see which answer works out. We vote for saving time!

When you're substituting numbers for variables, pick easy numbers to work with. Say that Jacob bought 10 pounds of flour for $3.50 a pound and 10 pounds of sugar for $4.50 a pound. That means that $x = 10$ and $s = 10$. Write this information on your test booklet. Jacob spent $35 on flour (10 times $3.50) and $45 on sugar (10 times $4.50). He also spent $18 for pans (3 times $6). The total cost is $98. Plug your made-up numbers into the answer choices to see which one equals 98.

Choice (C) is the only answer that equals $98 because $3.50(10) + $4.50(10) + $18.00 = $98.00.

13. E. To solve a series of equations, you must cancel out one of the variables. Because the question asks that you find y, it makes sense to cancel out x in order to isolate y. To do this, multiply the bottom equation by -2 and stack the two equations like this:

$$2x + 3y = 6$$
$$-6x + 2y = -16$$

When you add the equations, the x terms cancel, the y terms add to $5y$, and the sum of the right side of the equation is -10: $5y = -10$. When you solve for y, you get -2.

14. D. When converting a number in scientific notation, the easiest trick is to just move the decimal to the right the same number of places as the power of the 10. In this case, moving the decimal to the right -3 positions is the same as moving it to the left 3 positions. Write the number with extra zeros on each end and no decimal point in your test booklet. The number looks something like this:

00001540000

Now place the decimal in its original position between the 1 and the 5 and move it to the left 3 places to come up with the answer 0.00154. Then check your answer by moving the decimal to the right 3 places and see if you get the same number as in the original scientific notation number. You do!

15. B. To find the number of adult tickets sold, create a system of equations that models the given information. The equation for the total of 40 tickets sold could be $a + c = 40$, where a is the number of adult tickets sold and c is the number of children's tickets sold. The other equation is $\$8a + \$5c = \$251$ because the price of adult tickets times the number of adult tickets sold plus the price of children's tickets times the number of children's tickets sold equals the total cost of tickets sold. Because you want to find the number of adult tickets sold, it makes sense to cancel out the *c* variable and solve for *a*. First, multiply the first equation by -5 to get $-5a - 5c = -200$. Add that equation to $8a + 5c = 251$:

$$8a + 5c = 251$$
$$-2a - 5c = -200$$

Adding up these two equations, you find that $3a = 51$. When you divide both sides by 3, you find that $a = 17$.

16. **K.** First of all, you can tell from the graph that the parabola faces downward, so the x^2 term has to be negative. Right away, you can eliminate Choices (F) and (J). You can also tell that the graph has a vertical displacement of 3. Vertical displacement is indicated by the term that is added to or subtracted from the x^2 term. This means that you can get rid of Choice (G). You're down to Choices (H) and (K). The difference is that Choice (H) adds the 1 in parentheses and Choice (K) subtracts the 1. When the parabola moves in a positive direction horizontally, the number is subtracted from, not added to, *x* inside the parentheses. This means that the final answer is Choice (K).

You can check your answer by testing the vertex point in your equation to make sure it is valid. In this case, that point is (1, 3). When you plug the point into the equation in the answers, you get $3 = -(1-1)^2 + 3$ or $3 = 3$, which is true.

17. **B.** Solve the inequality just as you would an ordinary equation. Move all the constants to the right and all the *x* terms to the left. When you do, you end up with $-5x < 7$. Divide both sides by 5 to get a final solution for *x*: $x > -\dfrac{7}{5}$.

REMEMBER

When you divide both sides of an inequality by a negative value, you change the direction of the sign.

18. **J.** The standard form of the equation of a line is $y = mx + b$, where *m* is the slope and *b* is the y-intercept. You can tell from the graph that the y-intercept is at (0, 4) so $b = 4$. You can eliminate Choices (G) and (H) because when you solve them for *y*, they result in a *b* value of 3 instead of 4.

The next order of business is to determine the slope of the line by finding rise over run: $m = \dfrac{y_2 - y_1}{x_2 - x_1}$. The two given points on the graph are (0, 4) and (-3, 0). To find the slope, plug the coordinates into the equation: $m = \dfrac{0-4}{-3-0}$ or $m = \dfrac{4}{3}$. The only answer that results in a slope of $\dfrac{4}{3}$ when you solve for *y* is Choice (J).

19. **D.** When you add logs with the same base, you multiply the number being logged. So rewrite the question as $\log_6(9x) = 2$. Plug in your answer options for *x*. Choice (D) is correct because the product of 9 and 4 is 36, which is the value you get when you multiply 6 by itself two times.

TIP

The easiest way to solve logs is to know that the log base raised to the power of the answer equals the number being logged. In this problem, $6^2 = 9x$, so $x = 4$. Be careful to not get caught picking Choice (E), which adds rather than multiplies the numbers being logged.

20. **H.** Plug the values you know into the equation for volume of a circular cylinder: $V_c = \pi r^2 h$. To solve for *V*, you need the radius of the base and the height of the cylinder. The diameter is 10 cm, so the radius is half that, 5 cm. The height is 15 cm. The resulting solution is this:

$$V_c = (5\,cm)^2(15\,cm)\pi$$
$$V_c = (25\,cm)(15\,cm)\pi$$
$$V_c = 375\pi$$

TIP

After you memorize simple geometry formulas, questions that ask you to find the value of a shape's dimension will be some of the easiest and quickest to solve in the ACT Math section.

21. **A.** The original point A lies at $(-2, 4)$. Because the whole quadrilateral is reflected over the horizontal line $y = 2$, to find the reflected point A, you only need to reflect point A over the line $y = 2$. The x-coordinate of the point does not change because $y = 2$ is a horizontal line. You can eliminate Choices (B) and (C) because they don't contain x-coordinates of -2.

The original y value of point A is 4, which is 2 units above the line $y = 2$, so reflected point A is 2 units below the line $y = 2$. This makes the y value of reflected point A equal to 0 and the point $(-2, 0)$, which is Choice (A).

If you picked Choice (D), you reflected point A over the x-axis instead of the line $y = 2$.

22. **J.** This question is asking for all values of x that would make the quadratic equal to a number greater than 0. To solve it, factor the polynomial to give you $(x+5)(x-4)$. So the values for x that would make the expression equal to 0 are $x = -5$ and $x = 4$.

To find the values for x that make the expression greater than 0, consider that the expression is positive when both factors equal positive values or when both factors have negative values. The first factor is positive when $x > -5$ and the second factor is positive when $x > 4$, so both factors are positive when $x > 4$. At this point, you know the answer is Choice (J) because it's the only option that includes $x > 4$ and one other set of values for when the factors are both negative. Choice (K) doesn't take into consideration that the expression will be positive when both of its factors are negative.

TIP

Another way to approach this question is by substituting answer choices into the expression. Eliminate Choices (F) and (H) because although it's true that values over 20 make the solution greater than 0, so do some values that are less than or equal to 20. Choice (G) is wrong because values greater than 4 make the expression positive and some values less than 4 (say 3) make the expression negative. To evaluate Choice (J), try 5 and -6 for x in the expression. Both make its solution greater than 0, so Choice (J) is right and Choice (K) is wrong.

23. **C.** First, eliminate Choices (A) and (B). If Klaus gave money away, he started out with more than \$280. Then set up an equation. If Klaus gave 20% of his money and ended up with \$280, that \$280 is 80% of what he originally received. You can write 80% as 0.8 and *of* means multiply, so the equation is $0.8x = \$280$. To solve, divide each side by 0.8: $x = 350$. Choice (C) is correct.

Be sure not to just take 20% of the \$280. Remember, the \$280 already has been reduced by 20%, so 20% of that value is actually less than the amount that Klaus put in the bank.

24. **K.** This question is just a proportion in disguise! Set it up to solve for dollars. Fifty dollars for 20 gallons is the same as x dollars for 16 gallons: $\dfrac{\$50}{20\text{ gal}} = \dfrac{x}{16\text{ gal}}$.

Cross-multiply and solve:

$$(50)(16) = 20x$$
$$800 = 20x$$
$$40 = x$$

The correct answer is Choice (K).

25. D. The equation you use to find cosine is $\cos = \dfrac{\text{adjacent}}{\text{hypotenuse}}$. When you look at the figure, the side adjacent to angle C is a and the hypotenuse of triangle ABC is side b. So $\cos C = \dfrac{a}{b}$.

REMEMBER

You'll for sure encounter at least a couple trig questions that require you to apply the trig identities, so memorize the acronym SOH CAH TOA. Know it cold for test day.

26. G. To find the midpoint of a line segment, find the average of both the x and y-coordinates of the endpoints. The average of the x-coordinates is half of $-1 + 5$, which is 2. Eliminate any answer that doesn't have an x-coordinate of 2. That leaves you with Choices (G) and (J). Find the midpoint of the y-coordinates. Half of $3 - 5$ is -1. The answer is Choice (G).

If you picked Choice (F), you found the difference between the points instead of the sum.

27. D. To solve the equation for y, you must get y on its own side of the equation. First, subtract each side by 8 to get $x - 8 = 3y$. Then just divide both sides of the equation by 3 to get $\dfrac{x-8}{3} = y$, which is Choice (D).

If you forgot to also divide 8 by 3, you would have mistakenly selected Choice (A).

28. F. Label the whole line (from A to D) with a distance of 28, from A to C with 15, and from B to D with 18. It's easy to see that the distance from B to C is the overlapping portion of what you just labeled. Add the distance from A to C and the distance from B to D to get 33. Subtract 28 from 33 to get the distance of the overlap; the length between B and C is 5. Choice (F) is the answer.

TIP

Another way to solve this problem is to set up an equation. Call the distance between B and C x because that's the unknown. So the distance between A and B is $15 - x$ and the distance between C and D is $18 - x$. Set the sum of the three shorter segments equal to the longer length between A and D: $(15 - x) + x + (18 - x) = 28$. Simplify to get $33 - x = 28$ and you can see that x (the distance between B and C) equals 5.

29. C. To answer this question, set up a simple equation. Because Emma and Nadine both travel the same distance, you need to set up an equation where Emma's miles = Nadine's miles. Remember to convert minutes to hours because the units are in miles per hour rather than miles per minute. In hours, 40 minutes is $\dfrac{2}{3}$ of an hour. Multiply Emma's speed times the number of hours she spent in the car and set it equal to the number of hours Nadine spent in the car times Nadine's speed:

$$(45)\left(\dfrac{2}{3}\right) = (x)(1)$$
$$30 = x$$

Nadine's speed is 30 mph, which is Choice (C).

30. K. The fastest way to approach this problem is to notice that the measure of the perimeter is the same as the perimeter of a 23-by-18 rectangle. The length is $19 + 4$ or 23, and the width is $13 + 5$ or 18. So the perimeter is $(2)(23) + (2)(18)$, which is $46 + 36$ or 82. The answer is Choice (K).

Reading Test

1. C. First, go to the last paragraph to find Mrs. Kronborg's analogy. It appears in the last sentence right after the statement that Mrs. Kronborg knew talent meant practicing. She compares the need for a talented child to practice in the way that a child with measles needs to sleep. So a talented child *should* practice, and a child with measles *should* sleep. The answer that provides a similar *should* statement is Choice (C). A person with outdoor allergies *should* stay indoors.

Choice (A) is unlike the analogy because it mentions two separate skills — math and writing. For Choice (B), while it's obvious why a child with measles must be kept under blankets, it is decidedly less obvious why a beautiful child should be kept under close watch. So, that's probably not the best choice, either. Choice (D) uses *may* instead of *must*. *Must*, like *should*, is an absolution, while *may* is hypothetical. You can feel confident in selecting Choice (C).

TIP

You're supposed to choose the best answer out of the four options. To determine which is the best, use that secret weapon known as *POE*, or the process of elimination. By eliminating answers you know can't be right, you help isolate the answer that fits the best.

2. F. The second paragraph begins "It was in the summer that one really lived," so check there first. The author mentions fence painting in the third sentence, cottonwood trees in the fourth sentence, and the shedding of warm clothes for cotton at the end. So eliminate Choices (G), (H) and (J). By process of elimination, check Choice (F). The paragraph suggests that people see their neighbors, but it doesn't specifically say the neighbors are *new*. Choice (F) is correct.

3. H. Eliminate Choice (F), because the statement compares the way Mrs. Kohler treated Professor Wunsch to the way she treated her garden, and nothing in the passage suggests that there was anything undesirable about her garden. Eliminate Choice (G) because the paragraph goes on to discuss how Mrs. Kohler was successful in making the professor particularly clean and respectable — so she certainly wasn't trying in vain. Now, you're left with either Choice (H) or (J). Of the two, Choice (H) is better. The paragraph indicates that Mrs. Kohler helped get the professor in tip-top shape, but it doesn't provide clues to what would make up her idea of perfection. Stick with Choice (H).

4. A. Eliminate answers that contain elements that don't fit. Although the passage describes the garden as verdant, it doesn't suggest that it's the frequent rainfall that makes it green. Notice that the third paragraph describes the Kohler property as an open, sandy plain; it's unlikely that Moonstone receives frequent rainfall, so eliminate Choice (D). You can also easily get rid of Choice (C). The garden is a jungle of verdure, so it isn't best described as a barren sand gulch. Examine the remaining two choices for clues that would help you eliminate one. Choice (B) is true all the way up to the last word. Mrs. Kohler hasn't cultivated sage-brush in her garden, so the best answer must be Choice (A). The passage states that she hid and planned in her garden, and it's reasonable to assume that she found purpose in creating shade there.

TIP

Usually you can easily eliminate two answer choices. Then focus on the remaining two to find the one answer that contains an element that can't be justified by the passage. Eliminate that answer to discover the correct option.

5. D. The final paragraph of the passage discusses Thea's musical talent, and since *gifted* is a synonym for *talented*, Choice (D) is likely your answer. To be sure, though, take a look at the other possibilities. While the passage suggests Mrs. Kohler doesn't get out much, it doesn't indicate the same about Thea. You can't justify Choice (A). The first paragraph states that Thea has a favorite fairy tale, but it doesn't say she was particularly fond of fairy tales in general. Choice (C) is too much of a stretch. Choice (B) is true. Thea did study music with Professor Wunsch, but so did other children. Although Choice (B) is true, it doesn't show a way that Thea differed from other children. Stick with Choice (D).

Just because something in an answer choice is true doesn't necessarily mean it answers the question correctly.

An EXCEPT question requires you to find correct answers and then eliminate them. So, before you examine the answer choices, remind yourself to cross out "right" answers and choose the remaining "wrong" answer.

6. **H.** The opinions in Passage A are those of early 21st-century scholars and not necessarily the author. The author presents others' viewpoints without comment, so the primary tone is objective and explanatory. The best answer is Choice (H).

7. **G.** Don't worry if you're unfamiliar with the word in the question. Simply substitute the answer choices for *aetiology* in the passage to see which makes the most sense in context. The examples in the first sentence of Passage B are diagnoses and not word origins, so Choice (H) doesn't make sense. Although an abnormality is mentioned in one of the examples, none of the others mention it and the rest of the paragraph isn't about abnormalities. Choice (J) is wrong. To choose between controversy and causation, provided by the remaining two answer choices, examine the context of the paragraph. It mentions controversy, but the primary purpose of the paragraph addresses the causes of the disorders, so the aetiology lacking in the manual must be Choice (G).

8. **A.** To help you focus, analyze each answer one passage at a time. The psychiatrists mentioned in Passage A don't recognize a PTSD diagnosis and therefore, wouldn't consider it to be a debilitating condition. Eliminate Choice (B). The rest of the answers seem to work for Passage A, so consider the author of Passage B. The author doesn't feel that PTSD is a disorder of an altered baselines state, nor does the author mention politics, so Choices (C) and (D) don't work. The answer that fits both passages is Choice (A).

9. **D.** The author of Passage A claims that psychiatrists initially objected to the PTSD diagnosis in the third edition of the manual, so neither Choice (B) nor (C) is the exception. Passage B claims that few diagnoses in the manual listed causation, so Choice (A) is present and not an exception. Neither passage states that the manual is insufficient; the best answer is Choice (D).

10. **J.** Neither passage recommends additional research into PTSD, so Choice (G) is unlikely. Passage B isn't concerned with the speed of some professionals' PTSD diagnoses, so Choice (F) is wrong. Although both passages indicate that PTSD diagnosis is controversial, Passage B isn't concerned with its inclusion in the *DSM-III*; Choice (H) is out. Passage B states that "the presumed causal relationship between the stressor and PTSD. . .is complicated." Passage A suggests in the last paragraph that the types of stressors that could cause PTSD have broadened to a point where some medical professionals question the validity of the diagnosis. Therefore, both passages consider the exact relationship between stressors and PTSD to be controversial. Choose Choice (J).

When answering questions about the similarities and differences between two passages, examine the answer choices one passage at a time to help you focus and eliminate wrong answers more efficiently.

11. **A.** To answer this big idea question, apply the process of elimination. Rule out choices with information that is too specific. The passage discusses the idea in Choice (D) only in the fourth paragraph, so it's wrong. You should also get rid of answers that contain ideas that are too broad. Choice (B) focuses on the concept of positive change in general rather than

what makes for a good screenplay. Rule out Choice (C) because it's not true. The passage contains no warnings. The best answer has to be Choice (A). It ties the initial theme of what makes for a good film adaptation to the explanation of the life-changing mythological journey included throughout the rest of the passage.

TIP

For questions that ask you for the purpose or tone of an entire passage, choose answers that apply to the whole passage, not just part of it. Eliminate ideas that appear in only one or two of the paragraphs or that concern concepts that are more general than the passage's topic.

12. **J.** This question asks for the author's suggestion, which tells you that the correct answer is implied rather than directly stated. In the second paragraph, the author makes a primary observation about inner growth and change — that it means letting go of the familiar and risking the unknown. The answer that paraphrases this idea best is Choice (J). The author states that inner growth is healthy, so you can eliminate Choice (F) based on its first two words. Even though the rest of this first answer choice seems pretty good, don't ignore its implication that inner growth is unhealthy. Read Choice (H) carefully; it actually contradicts the notion that inner growth requires change. The second paragraph says that inner growth requires courage but not the courage to stay the same. The last line of the paragraph conveys that remaining static isn't a requirement for inner growth but instead an obstacle to achieving it. Choice (G) may seem correct at first, but the passage only says that experiencing myth in film may assist with the dilemma of whether to risk change. It doesn't say inner growth requires viewing films. The answer must be Choice (J). The second paragraph states that inner growth requires sacrificing the old and familiar and risking the unknown and uncertain. The last paragraph quotes Campbell's claim that human fantasies tend to tie back to the human spirit, so you can reasonably conclude that comfortable fantasies are included in the "old and familiar," and uncharted territory is another way of alluding to the unknown.

13. **F.** Choice (F) is essentially a rephrasing of a sentence that appears in the middle of the final paragraph: "Mythology . . . provides a means for other people to experience the hero's transformation." That sounds good, but check the other answers to be sure. A protagonist people can easily identify with isn't one of the elements of a good story listed in the first paragraph, so Choice (G) is out. Eliminate Choice (H); the second paragraph contrasts the tangibility of inner and outer change but doesn't state that one is more important than the other. The first paragraph doesn't include a widely loved story as one of the criteria for a film adaptation's success, so Choice (J) is out. Choice (F) is best.

14. **F.** The passage references Joseph Campbell in the third paragraph, so start there. It states that the purpose of ritual is to provide transformation that demands changes in conscious and unconscious patterns. That sounds most like Choice (F). Choice (G) references difficult thresholds in general, but the reference is specifically to thresholds of transformation. The paragraph doesn't suggest that ritual forces anything, nor does it mention fantasy. So Choices (H) and (J) are wrong, and the best answer is Choice (F).

15. **G.** From the first paragraph, you know that Seger is an author of a book about adaptation and that the adaptation is likely from literature to film. Therefore, she's most likely a film script consultant. Pick Choice (G).

16. **D.** While the roles of bacteria, or Choice (C), are indeed discussed, this discussion appears in only a small part of the passage and not until about halfway through. If bacteria were the main purpose of the passage, one could expect that they would be mentioned in the very first paragraph — so eliminate Choice (C). Similarly, while some attention is given to the earth's changing temperatures, or Choice (A), there isn't nearly enough to have temperature change be the passage's central or primary focus. So, you're down to either Choice (B) or (D). Of the two, Choice (D) is broader and more all-encompassing and better summarizes

the passage in its entirety. While the author notes that "If there is anything that has been overlooked more than another it is our atmosphere," he really only devotes the first couple paragraphs to discussing why the atmosphere is overlooked. When you examine the passage in its entirety, Choice (D) is the strongest choice.

17. **G.** The correct answer is Choice (G). The passage claims that rain is "accounted for only by the dust," which means that the rain exists because the dust exists. You can't conclude, however, that this statement means that rain is the only element dust accounts for. Choices (H), and (J) are all mentioned by the author in Paragraph 7, and Choice (F) is mentioned in Paragraph 8.

18. **F.** While both Choice (G) and Choice (H) are ways in which dust affects the earth, neither is discussed in such a way that would suggest the author considers them dust's greatest role. So, your answer is either Choice (F) or (J). Choice (J) sounds like something the author might say about atmosphere rather than dust, and furthermore, the author essentially paraphrases Choice (F) at the start of Paragraph 8. Choice (F) is correct.

19. **D.** While Choice (A) is an assertion made by the author, he doesn't appear to consider this fact an absurdity, so go ahead and knock that one out of contention. Eliminate Choice (B) for the same reason. Take a closer look at the remaining choices. Choice (C) is indeed noted by the author in the passage's final paragraph, but it is done so in a matter-of-fact manner, suggesting that the author doesn't consider it an absurdity. Only in his discussion of rain and dust does he use the word *absurdities*, so you may confidently select Choice (D).

20. **G.** To answer this question correctly, look for clues in the context. The line in question states, "It is thanks to this thin layer of gases that we are protected from that fraction of sunheat which, however trifling when compared with the whole, would otherwise be sufficient to fry us all in a second." So you're likely looking for a word that means something close to "a small part." Thus, *insignificant* is the strongest answer. To be sure, though, take a look at the others. Choice (F), *shallow*, certainly doesn't mean a small part, so knock that one out of contention. Eliminate Choice (J) because *novel* means new, not small. As for Choice (H), *trifling* could mean silly, but try substituting the word *trifling* in the paragraph with *silly*. Does it make sense to say the earth receives a silly fraction of sunheat? No, so Choice (G) is correct.

Science Test

1. **D.** The question points you to the data for Site 1 on the table. It asks you to determine the relationship, if any, between temperature and conductivity. Don't assume that the temperatures increase as you move down the chart. Note that the first two temperatures are both 23 but the conductivity for both entries is very different. So there isn't an obvious relationship between the two and Choice (D) is the best answer.

The answer that states there's no apparent relationship or that data is insufficient is often the last answer and may be correct. So don't be afraid to pick it. Don't assume there must be a relationship.

2. **F.** The table doesn't have a category for number of impurities, so you need to read a bit of the text to determine which column gives you the information you need to assess purity. The first sentences indicate that removing ions is a way to purify water and that conductivity and ion content are directly related — the more ions a solution has, the higher its conductivity. So use the conductivity column on the table to assess the sites' relative purity. The site with the lowest conductivity is Site 1. Its average conductivity is around 200 as compared to 870 at Site 2 and 620 at Site 3. Pick Choice (F).

You know that Choice (J) can't be right because the conductivity averages for Sites 1 and 3 are very different.

3. **A.** This question provides new information — that drinking water's conductivity usually ranges between 50 and 500. Use it to evaluate the table. The only site with conductivity levels between 50 and 500 is Site 1. The answer has to be Choice (A).

This question was very similar to the second question. Don't be thrown off if you think the ACT Science questions test you more than once on the same general concept. They do it all the time.

4. **H.** To extrapolate for this question, use the table to find the average conductivity that's closest to 500. Site 2's average at about 620 is higher than 500, and Site 1's average at about 200 is much lower. The average species richness for Site 1 is 10.7 and for Site 2 is 4.9. The answer has to lie between those two values. So pick Choice (H).

5. **B.** Data are correlated when you can determine a relationship between them. Notice that for fall on three sites the temperatures were roughly the same. Yet species richness varied among the sites. So temperature isn't correlated to species richness, and you can eliminate Choices (A) and (C). Check conductivity. It appears from the average figures that lower conductivity means greater species richness, so those data are correlated. The answer is Choice (B).

6. **H.** The passage indicates that species richness was collected from freshwater sites. It then explains that based on the collection invertebrate specimens were counted and identified. The logical means of collecting invertebrates is nets, Choice (H). The passage doesn't associate temperature, pH, or weight with species richness, so the other answers must be wrong.

7. **D.** The passage doesn't test behaviors of saltwater fish, so Choice (A) is incorrect. The setup for Experiment 1 lists the types of aggressive behaviors the scientists viewed as a fact rather than a question to answer through experimentation; eliminate Choice (B). The two experiments include gender and size considerations in their setup, but the main difference between them is the relative size of the intruder fish and the focal fish. Experiment 1 established the number of aggressive behaviors presented when one intruder and focal fish are of similar size. The second experiment provides information the scientists can use to determine whether the number of aggressive behaviors changes when they vary the comparative size of intruders and focal fish for a larger number of fish. The scientists do not mix the sexes of the intruders and focal fish, so Choice (C) isn't correct. The scientists must be primarily concerned with how the relative size of the intruder affects the number of aggressive behaviors in the focal fish. Choice (D) is best.

8. **H.** The question directs you to Experiment 1, so focus on the data in Table 1. Before you do, however, take a look at the answer choices. All but the first begin with large male as the one with the highest aggression. Notice that in the column for large fish, the males have more aggressive behaviors than the females, so eliminate Choice (F). The second entry in the remaining choices is either large female or medium male. Check Table 1 to see which has more aggressive behaviors. The large female has 11 and the medium male has 18, so the male is more aggressive and Choice (G) is wrong. Choice (H) and (J) differ in the order of the last two fish. The large female has one more aggressive behavior than the small male, so based on the table, the answer has to be Choice (H).

9. **B.** Use information from both tables to answer this question. You know from answering Question 6 about Experiment 1 that male fish are generally more aggressive than female fish, so eliminate Choices (A) and (C). Check Table 2 to see whether the findings change in the second experiment. The males are generally more aggressive in the second experiment, too, so the answer has to be Choice (B).

10. **G.** To answer this question, you determine how the experiments differed based on what's true for Experiment 2. First, run through the answer choices to eliminate options that aren't true about the independent variables in Experiment 2. The number of days didn't vary in Experiment 2, so eliminate Choice (J). The researchers were testing for aggression, so Choice (H) wasn't an independent variable and must be wrong. The gender and relative size of the intruders varied in Experiment 2. The difference between the two experiments, though, was that Experiment 2 varied the comparable sizes of intruders to focal fish. This variation didn't occur in Experiment 1, so the best answer is Choice (G).

11. **D.** The columns in Table 2 vary the size of the intruder, so that element must be important in determining aggressive behavior. Eliminate Choices (A) and (B) because neither mentions size of intruder. Then you just need to determine whether the gender of the focal fish was another factor. The table rows delineate male and female data, and the text tells you that the gender of the focal fish determined the gender of the intruder. So gender must also be important, and the answer must be Choice (D).

12. **F.** Read the introductory text to discover that aggression allows the fish to protect their young. In both experiments, bigger fish meant more aggression for both genders. So the best answer is one that pairs the fish with the most aggressive behaviors. From Table 1, you learn that the medium male and large female would have about 32 aggressive behaviors between them. The large male and small female would have about 29 aggressive behaviors. So get rid of Choice (G). The other answers contain smaller males than Choice (G), so you can eliminate them as well. The answer is Choice (F).

REMEMBER

Don't overthink this question. You're choosing the best answer and are given only the number of aggressive behaviors and time spent in aggressive behaviors to evaluate. Between the two experiments, you see that the number of aggressive behaviors correlates directly with the number of minutes engaged in those behaviors. So the combination that produces the most aggressive behaviors has to be better than any other answer with a smaller number of behaviors.

13. **A.** Translate the data in the table to a bar graph. Table 2 shows the number of minutes spent in aggression. Bigger fish spent more time than smaller fish and males more than females, so pick the graph that best reflects this trend. All graphs show more time for males, so focus on size.

Eliminate answers that show higher bars for smaller intruders. So Choices (B) and (D) are out. You can also eliminate Choice (C) because it shows time for equal intruders higher than for larger intruders. The answer has to be Choice (A).

14. **F.** The question directs you to Researcher 1, so start there. Researcher 1's overall opinion on GMOs is positive, so Choice (J) is unlikely. Choice (G) doesn't describe benefits, so eliminate it. Choices (F) and (H) are benefits, but the researcher never says that GMOs increase nutritional values. The statement is that they haven't been shown to have fewer nutrients than organics, but that's not the same as having more nutritional value. Choice (F) is the best answer.

15. **B.** The first researcher is generally positive about GMOs and the second is generally negative, so they are unlikely to agree on much. Eliminate Choice (A) because both researchers say the opposite — decreasing pesticides is good for the environment. Researcher 2 states that the taste and quality of GMOs is inferior to organics, so Choice (C) is out. Researcher 1 mentions allergies, but Researcher 2 doesn't, so Choice (D) is wrong. Both researchers state that no correlation exists between health problems and GMOs, so the best answer is Choice (B).

16. **F.** Researcher 2 states directly that no correlation exists between health problems and GMOs, so Choice (J) is out. The first sentence of Researcher 2's paragraph states that pests become resistant to GMOs, but that doesn't necessarily mean that their use decreases naturally occurring pest reducers or increases the use of harmful pesticides. So Choices (G) and (H) are out, and by process of elimination, Choice (F) is correct. The last disadvantage mentioned by Researcher 2 is that plant pollen travels large distances, which means organic foods are contaminated by GMOs.

17. **D.** Choice (A) is mentioned by Researcher 2 but not Researcher 1. Choice (B) is mentioned by neither. And Researcher 1 specifically states that GMOs do not have reduced nutritional value. Eliminate Choices (A), (B), and (C). The first researcher mentions the possibility of increased allergies in the last sentence of the opinion. So the answer has to be Choice (D).

18. **F.** The second researcher mentions planting a variety of species, using natural repellants such as ladybugs, and increasing community farms as ways of reducing pesticides. Eliminate all answers but Choice (F). This researcher warns that GMOs can pollinate organic crops, so it's unlikely that he would advocate for growing some GMOs.

19. **C.** A link suggests a cause-and-effect relationship. Researcher 2 discusses the rise of community gardens as possible ways to reduce pesticide use and put less strain on food-producing corporations. Neither is necessarily linked to GMO use. Although the researcher states that pests become resistant to GMOs more quickly, he doesn't state that pesticide use increases as a result. The researcher isn't impressed with the food quality of GMOs, so the best answer is Choice (C).

20. **G.** Scan the options. The graphs show several relationships concerning GMOs and pesticide use, and you're supposed to choose the one that represents what Researcher 1 thinks. The first few sentences of Researcher 1's opinion indicate an inverse relationship between GMOs and pesticide use. As GMOs increase, pesticides decrease. So you can eliminate Choice (F). Choice (H) is out because Researcher 1 states that increased use of GMOs increases crop yields. Researcher 1 agrees that increased pesticide use creates increased harm to the environment, but so does Researcher 2, so Choice (J) is consistent with the opinions of both researchers. The best answer is Choice (G). Researcher 2 isn't convinced that GMOs directly cause a decrease in pesticide use because pests become resistant to GMO plants, which suggests that pesticides would eventually be necessary with GMOs as well.

Writing Test

If you wrote the optional essay for this test, check it over and make sure your essay contains these necessary features:

>> **A clear position:** Did you take a stand and stick to it? Remember that which side you take isn't a big deal. How well you support your position makes or breaks your essay. You should take only a few seconds to choose which side to argue before you start writing.

>> **A clear understanding of the complexity of the issue:** Top essays include a careful analysis of possible positions to weigh the pros and cons of all and arrive at the best possible solution.

>> **A strong thesis:** Did you create a thesis that answers the question posed by the prompt and sets up your essay? Try to slip in some of the wording from the prompt. Make sure your thesis introduces the two or three main points you use to back up your stand on the issue.

>> **A steady focus:** Every element of your essay should be about your thesis. Make sure you didn't stray off topic.

>> **Good organization:** We know it sounds boring, but your essay must have an introduction, body, and conclusion. Make sure you devote each paragraph in the body to a discussion of one of your two or three main supporting points. Check out the tips in Block 2 to help you evaluate the organization of your essay.

>> **Excellent examples:** Professional essay readers really love to see creative, descriptive examples that strengthen your points. Vivid details draw readers in and endear them to your writing prowess.

>> **Clear and interesting writing:** Check your essay for sentence structure variety, precise word choice, and impeccable spelling, grammar, and punctuation.

Sample response

The issue of whether elderly drivers should be forced to retake driver's tests once they reach a certain age is indeed polarizing. Studies show that drivers' ability to drive safely diminishes once they reach a particular age, but some believe that forcing drivers to reapply is offensive and a form of age discrimination. Despite the potential for offense, requiring that drivers test after a certain age is necessary to maintain public safety.

Diminished vision and decreased reaction time are common effects of the aging process, and they are also common consequences of drinking and driving. No one argues that drinking and driving is dangerous, so why would we accept the same dangerous behaviors in our elderly population? Laws are enacted to ensure public safety. People shouldn't be able to drive while impaired whether that impairment is from taking substances or advanced age.

Given the increased safety mandatory testing would ensure, issues of age discrimination don't hold up. Simply put, some things require more attention as we age. Take a mammogram, for example. Most young women aren't having them performed regularly because they aren't as likely to develop breast cancer as older women, but the procedure is a necessary step to ensure safety as women age. Discrimination is justified when the circumstances result in benefit. If forcing older populations to retest once they reach a certain age is age discrimination against the elderly, then allowing those over age 62 to receive social security benefits is discriminatory against those under 62. Allowing those over 21 to consume alcohol is not discriminatory to those who have yet to reach the age of 21. Some age discrimination is necessary when taking into consideration the different circumstances for different age groups.

People change as a result of the aging process. Creating laws that are appropriate for these changes to maintain safety is logical and justifies issues of age discrimination. Having elderly drivers reapply for driver's licenses is necessary to maximize safety and allow the greatest number of people to enjoy full, long, and healthy lives.

Block 5

Ten Tips for the Night Before Your Test

I t's the night before you take the ACT and you want to do your best! This block gives you ten tips to help feel super confident when you walk into the ACT testing room.

Know Your Time-Management Strategies

You probably already know that the ACT is a timed test. When the time is up, you can't answer any more questions or go back and review your answers. It pays to go over your time management strategies:

>> Know how much time you have for each question.

>> Mark your answers in your booklet before you mark them in your answer sheet. This will save you time if you mess up your answer sheet and need to redo it. And you'll save time reviewing your answers if you don't have to switch back and forth from your booklet to the answer sheet.

>> Skip the hard questions. If you don't know an answer, remember that you don't get bonus points for answering harder questions. They all count the same. If you have time, go back to the hard question at the end or just guess.

See Block 1 for more specifics about managing your time.

Review Strategies for Analyzing and Answering Questions

The ACT is mostly about testing what you know about certain topics, but you'll do better with a few test-taking strategies in your back pocket. Remember these tips:

» **Eliminate answers.** Unlike life, the ACT is a multiple-choice test and the possible answers will be presented to you. Some of them will be obviously wrong, so you can strike them out and focus on the more probable answers.

» **Read actively to maintain your focus.** This tip is helpful when you're reading passages. Write a word or phrase next to each paragraph that summarizes what it's about. In addition to helping you stay focused, these notes can help you find information in the passage that will help you answer questions that ask about specific details you read.

» **Review your answers.** Focus on the easy and medium level questions because they're the ones you're most likely to get correct.

See Block 1 for more about these strategies.

Review Your Practice Test Materials

One of the best ways to prepare for the ACT is to take a practice test. Save that work, and you have an easy way to review what you got right and what you need to review the night before so it's fresh in your mind. Block 4 is an abbreviated practice test with explanations of the answers.

Practice Your Stress-Coping Strategies

If you, like many test takers all over the world, struggle with test-taking anxiety, this tip is a must. Know that you've got this and make and practice a specific plan for managing your anxiety if catches you off-guard during the test. Block 1 provides specific anxiety-reducing strategies if you need them.

Plan for Arriving on Time

You don't want to arrive to the test-taking site late or stressed because you were almost late. Before the test, make sure you know exactly how you'll get to the test site and plan to get there at least 15 to 20 minutes early so you have some extra time in case anything goes wrong with your well-laid travel plans.

Also, you can set multiple alarms on your phone: Set two for whenever you need to wake up so you have a backup in case you turn off your alarm in your sleep. Set another alarm for 15 minutes before you need to leave and one more for the moment you need to leave your house in order to get to the test center on time.

Lay Out Comfortable Clothes

Taking a test is not comfortable. The chair you sit in may not be comfortable. Your clothes can be very comfortable. Wear your most comfortable outfit and dress in layers in case the test room is hotter or colder than you expect it to be.

Have Your Picture ID and Admission Ticket Ready

To be admitted to the testing room, you must have a picture ID and an admission ticket. Know exactly where they are and put them in a spot that will help you remember to bring them with you.

Check Your Calculator and Batteries

You can use a calculator on the ACT, but your calculator will do you no good if it doesn't work. Check that your calculator has working batteries, or even better, pop new batteries into your calculator the night before so you know it'll work through the whole test.

Visualize Success!

You've prepared for this test, and you're going to do your very best. Imagine yourself walking to the test center with plenty of time to spare, your ID and ticket in hand. Imagine working through each exam, recognizing the questions and what you need to do. Imagine yourself checking your answers so you have the best chance of getting your desired score. You've got this!

Get a Good Night's Sleep

Don't try to slog through almost four hours of questions on a few hours' sleep. You'll do your best on the ACT if you have a good night's sleep. Plan for the calmest night you can imagine the night before the test and do something relaxing right before you go to bed.

Lay Out Comfortable Clothes

Have Your Picture ID and Admission Ticket Ready

Check Your Calculator and Batteries

Visualize Success!

Get a Good Night's Sleep

Index

About the Authors

Lisa Zimmer Hatch, MA, and **Scott A. Hatch, JD,** have been preparing teens and adults to excel on standardized tests, gain admission to colleges of their choice, and secure challenging, lucrative professional careers since 1987. For more than 30 years, they have administered their award-winning standardized test-preparation and professional career courses for live college lectures, online forums, and other formats through more than 300 universities worldwide.

Lisa and Scott have taught students internationally through live lectures, online forums, and independent study opportunities. They have written the curriculum for all formats, and their books have been translated for international markets. Together they have authored numerous law and standardized test-prep texts, including *GMAT for Dummies, LSAT For Dummies, 1,001 ACT Practice Problems For Dummies, SAT II U.S. History For Dummies, SAT II Biology For Dummies, Catholic High School Entrance Exams For Dummies,* and *Paralegal Career For Dummies* (John Wiley & Sons, Inc.).

Lisa is currently an independent educational consultant and the president of College Primers, where she applies her expertise to guiding high school and college students through the testing, admissions, and financial aid processes. She dedicates herself to helping students gain admission to the colleges or programs that best fit their goals, personalities, and finances. She graduated with honors in English from the University of Puget Sound and received a master's degree in humanities with a literature emphasis from California State University. She has completed the UCLA College Counseling Certificate Program and is a member of the Higher Education Consultants Association (HECA) where she serves on the Professional Development committee.

Scott received his undergraduate degree from the University of Colorado and his Juris Doctor from Southwestern University School of Law. He is listed in *Who's Who in California* and *Who's Who Among Students in American Colleges and Universities* and was named one of the Outstanding Young Men of America by the United States Junior Chamber (Jaycees). He was also a contributing editor to the *Judicial Profiler* and *Colorado Law Annotated* and has served as editor of several national award-winning publications. His current books include *A Legal Guide to Probate and Estate Planning* and *A Legal Guide to Family Law,* which are the inaugural texts in B & B Publication's Learn the Law series.

Publisher's Acknowledgments

Executive Editor: Lindsay Lefevere
Compiling Editor: Rebecca Huehls
Editor: Elizabeth Kuball

Production Editor: Saikarthick Kumarasamy
Cover Design: Wiley
Cover Image: © bortonia/Getty Images